SECURITY OPTIONS STRATEGY

BOOKS BY ALBERT I. A. BOOKBINDER

INVESTMENT DECISION-MAKING
SECURITY OPTIONS STRATEGY

Security Options Strategy

by

ALBERT I. A. BOOKBINDER, Ph.D.

Professor of Economics
City University of New York

PROGRAMMED PRESS
2301 Baylis Avenue
Elmont, N. Y. 11003

SECURITY OPTIONS STRATEGY
Copyright © 1976 by ALBERT I. A. BOOKBINDER

This publication is designed to provide accurate and authoritative information regarding the subject matter covered. It is sold with the understanding that the publisher is not engaged in rendering legal, accounting or other professional service. If legal advice or other expert assistance is required, the services of a competent professional person should be sought.

From a Declaration of Principles jointly adopted by a Committee of the American Bar Association and a Committee of Publishers.

Library of Congress Cataloging in Publication Data

BOOKBINDER, ALBERT I. A.
SECURITY OPTIONS STRATEGY

Includes bibliographical references and index.
1. Put and call transactions   2. Hedging (Finance)   1. Title

ISBN 0-916106-01-2 (cloth binding)
ISBN 0-916106-02-0 (paperback)

Library of Congress Catalog Card No. 76-46120
Printed in the United States of America

AGAIN FOR S. B.
WITH LOVE

PREFACE

This book is not intended for the "average investor." SECURITY OPTIONS STRATEGY may be used by the serious investor, the sophisticated speculator and especially by the professional money manager as a basic textbook.

SECURITY OPTIONS STRATEGY shows how put and call options can be used to minimize risk and raise the rate of return on investment. It also scrutinizes the pitfalls of various strategies utilized in either buying or writing options.

The original manuscript was edited by Dr. Mary M. McDougall, Assistant Professor of Economics at the City University of New York. In addition to the manuscript, the practical applications of the strategies and tactics were reviewed by Maxwell Ohlman, Adjunct Professor of the Graduate School of Business of Fordham University. Dr. Victor R. Farhi, Professor of Economics and Finance of Fairleigh Dickinson University, scrutinized the mathematical formulae as well as the original manuscript. The final manuscript was reviewed by Leon Pomerance, the Chairman of the Board of Directors of the Chicago Board Options Exchange. Dr. Leon Kilbert, Vice President and Director of Chase Investors Management Corporation, reviewed the final manuscript in its entirety.

Above all, my wife, Sarah, merits my appreciation for diligently designing and editing the book.

ALBERT I. A. BOOKBINDER

Elmont, New York
September 1975

CONTENTS

EXHIBITS

TABLES

SECURITY OPTIONS STRATEGY

CHAPTER 1

Option Contracts

Option contracts originated some 4,000 years ago. When Jacob wished to marry Rachel, he agreed to pay Laban seven years labor as the premium for a call on his daughter's hand. This price paid by the bridegroom to the father of the bride was an essential element of virtually all early Hebrew marriage contracts.[1]

Options to buy or sell securities serve many useful purposes and take various forms. The two basic forms of option contracts are puts and calls. A put is an option giving the holder the right to sell specified stock (usually 100 shares) at a stated price at any time within the contract period. In contrast, a call is an option giving the holder the right to buy certain stock at a stated price at any time within the contract period. A put or call is sold by an option writer for a cash consideration commonly called the premium or option price.

[1] The Bible—Genesis 29.

1

The call option writer is obliged to sell the stock at the contract or striking price if and when the call is exercised by the option holder, no matter how high the market price of the stock actually climbs. The put option writer, on the other hand, must buy the stock at the exercise or striking price if and when the put is exercised by the option holder, regardless of how low the market price of the stock actually falls.

A put or call is exercised at the discretion of the option holder. Whether or not an option is exercised depends on the movement of the market price of the stock after the option contract is written. If the price of the underlying stock declines and is not higher than the striking price, a call option is simply allowed to expire without being exercised. Similarly, a put option is permitted to lapse unexercised, if the market price of the underlying stock rises and is not lower than the striking price.

In addition to these basic put and call option contracts, certain combinations of these options as well as variations in contract terms may be used. A "straddle" is a combination of a put and a call exercisable on the same stock at the same price. A "spread" is a variation of the straddle in which the put and the call are exercisable at different prices or at different expiration dates. A "strip" represents a call plus two puts, while a "strap" consists of one put plus two calls.

Among other types of options are non-negotiable executive stock options generally issued to officers of corporations and also warrants and convertible securities. Since employee options are not negotiable instruments, they cannot be freely traded in a public market. A warrant is a long-term call on shares of the underlying stock. A convertible bond is really a bond plus a long-term call option exercisable by an exchange of the bond for the underlying shares within the option period. Similarly, a convertible preferred stock is a preferred stock plus a long-term call option exercisable by an exchange of the preferred stock for the underlying

2

shares of common stock within the option period. Whereas warrants and convertible securities are available on only some stocks, put and call options may be bought and sold on almost all common stocks.

The Put and Call Brokers and Dealers Association requires that an option traded in the over-the-counter market be endorsed by a New York Stock Exchange member firm, guaranteeing contract performance by the option writer. But an option listed on an organized securities exchange needs no endorsement by any member firm, because contract performance is effectively guaranteed by the Options Clearing Corporation. The endorsement or guarantee makes an option a fully negotiable instrument transferable like any other security.

Option contracts traded in the over-the-counter market usually provide that the exercise or striking price will be reduced by the value of any distributions received on the stock during the life of the option. In the case of listed call options traded on an organized securities exchange, the contracts provide for adjustment to the exercise price in the event of dividends (other than ordinary cash dividends), distributions, stock splits or recapitalizations with respect to the underlying stock. Unlike options traded in the over-the-counter market, no adjustment is made to any of the terms of Exchange Traded Options to reflect the declaration or payment of ordinary cash dividends. However, if an option holder files an exercise notice with the Options Clearing Corporation prior to an ex-dividend date for an ordinary cash dividend, the exercising option holder is entitled to that dividend even though the writer to whom the exercise is assigned may receive actual notice of such assignment after the ex-dividend date.

PREMIUM

The option price or premium is the amount the buyer pays for an option and is what the writer receives in return for granting the option. The premium is all-important in an option transaction, since it can mean the difference between a profit or loss for the buyer or seller.

In the over-the-counter option market, most puts and calls are written at the current market price and the amount of the premium varies with the price of the underlying stock. On typical six-month call options, the premium paid by buyers averages 14% of the price of the stock, while the premium received by writers comes to some 12%. The two-point spread in these percentages between what the buyer pays and what the writer receives represents the 15% average mark-up by over-the-counter option dealers.[2]

The premium also varies with the type of option contract, the length of the option period and the volatility of the underlying stock. The premium for a six-month option is generally two and one-half times what it would be on a 30-day contract on the same security, nearly 50% greater than a 90-day option and hardly more than two-thirds that of a 12-month contract. As a rule, the premium tends to be higher on low-priced and volatile stocks. On six-month options, writers generally get premiums averaging 9% of the price of the stock on puts, 12% on calls and 20% on straddle contracts. Thus, straddles obtain the largest premiums, while the calls get larger premiums than put options.

CONVERSION

Call options are higher priced than puts, because there is generally greater demand for calls than puts. On the other hand, most option writers prefer to sell straddles, because these dual options command considerably larger premiums than either simple puts or calls. Straddles, moreover, have smaller margin requirements and receive favored tax treatment. For margin purposes, the same stock covers both sides of a straddle. For tax purposes, unlike in-

[2] U.S. Securities and Exchange Commission, Report on Put and Call Options, 1961.

4

dividual puts or calls, income from the lapsed part of a straddle is treated as a short-term capital gain rather than ordinary income. Furthermore, it is extremely unlikely that both sides of the straddle will be exercised. Should both sides be exercised, the writer's investment position in the stock will remain unchanged and he will be ahead by the amount of the premium received.

Since option buyers are interested chiefly in calls rather than in puts and writers prefer to sell straddles, this seeming disparity between an excess supply of puts and an excess demand for calls is resolved by a conversion practice. The put and call dealer, who has buyers for two calls on the same stock, purchases a straddle from a writer and then exchanges the put for a call issued by an option converter. Simultaneously, the converter buys the underlying stock on the Exchange. Then if the call is not exercised, the converter disposes of the stock by exercising the put.

Occasionally, calls are converted into puts. The converter accomplishes this by simultaneously writing a put in exchange for a call with the option dealer and selling the stock short. Then if the put is exercised, the converter covers his short position with the put stock. If the put is not exercised, the short position is covered by exercising the call he holds.

Converting a put option into a call or a call option into a put is virtually a riskless practice by a small number of sophisticated New York Stock Exchange member firms. A converter charges the option dealer a fee which exceeds the brokers' call money interest rate on the capital invested in the underlying stock for the life of the option plus the cost of two floor brokerage fees. Capitalizing on the spread between put and call premiums, this practically riskless investment with a virtually certain return for converters is factually a form of arbitrage. Consequently, this possibility of option arbitrage tends to establish an effective ceiling on the spread between put and call premiums.[3]

---

[3] Hans R. Stoll, "The Relationship between Put and Call Option Prices", Journal of Finance, Dec. 1969, pp. 801-824.

OPTION BUYING

Virtually anyone can deal in options, but most buyers of puts and calls are individuals, not institutional investors. In some states, financial institutions may write options, but are prohibited from purchasing puts and calls. In the face of legal obstacles, nevertheless, there is increasing interest in option buying by some institutions, notably hedge funds.

Basically, an option is bought for the purpose of limiting the amount of loss in a security investment or speculation, while giving the purchaser unlimited opportunity for profit. While the possible profit may be relatively unlimited, the potential loss is limited to the cost of the option and that amount is known in advance.

Although puts and calls are commonly purchased for speculation on a small amount of capital, they may be used as a hedge or insurance against a security position. To protect an existing security position, puts must be bought against a long position and calls must be purchased against a short position. A bullish or optimistic speculator may buy a call and a bearish speculator could purchase a put. A speculator anticipating considerable volatility of the price of the related stock in either or both directions could buy a straddle.

CALLS

Many security traders prefer to buy call options, because calls can control a large amount of stock with a relatively small amount invested, so that they get greater percentage profit potential than by purchasing securities outright or even on margin. At the same time, the potential loss is limited to the cost of the option, without limiting the opportunity for possible profits. A call can be used for speculation on a small amount of capital, protection of a short position or in-and-out trading at limited risk.

The speculative use of a call anticipates a profit from the price fluctuations in the underlying stock. Suppose a trader considering the purchase of U.S. Steel wishes to limit his risk. He buys a 3-month call on U.S. Steel at 40 for a $400 premium. If the stock rises to 50 by the end of the three-month period, he would exercise the call and then sell the shares. His account would show:

Sale of 100 U.S. Steel @ 50	$5,000
Purchase of 100 U.S. Steel @ 40	4,000
Gain on stock	1,000
Cost of call	400
Profit (before commissions)	$ 600

Had this trader bought the stock for cash instead of exercising the call option, his gain would have been $1,000 (less commissions) on a $4,000 investment, or a return of 25%. By buying the call, however, his gain was $600 on an investment of $400, or a return of 150%. But if the price of the stock had dropped, he would have allowed his option to expire unexercised and his loss would have been limited to the $400 cost of the call option.

This example illustrates the speculative use of a call for its leverage potential. Since an option premium is substantially less than the cost of the underlying stock, a given amount of cash can buy options covering a much larger quantity of shares than could be bought directly. In this way, a call can benefit from a rise in the price of the stock to a much greater extent than the outright purchase of the stock. However, if the stock does not appreciate during the life of the option, the entire investment in the option would be lost. Unlike the direct purchase of the shares, a call buyer cannot wait for an upturn in the price of the stock beyond the option's expiration date. Furthermore, a call does not become profitable until the stock appreciates in price by more than the amount of the premium paid for the option.

A call option can provide protection against unlimited loss in connection with a short sale, since this option gives the holder the

7

right to buy the underlying stock at a fixed price. If the market price of the stock remains unchanged or declines, the option holder would lose the amount of the premium paid. Any gain on the short sale would be reduced by that amount. If the price of the stock should rise, however, the short seller would be protected against a substantial loss by exercising the call option and delivering the called stock against the short position.

To illustrate, suppose a trader simultaneously sells stock short and buys a call at 50 for a $400 premium. Should the price of the stock rise to 75, the short sale could be covered by buying the stock at the call price of 50. Instead of covering the short position at a $2,500 loss, the call enables this option holder to limit his loss (before commissions) to the $400 cost of the option.

A call option also makes possible in-and-out trading opportunities at limited risk, since stocks seldom move in a straight line but do fluctuate. Hence, a trader who buys a call may have a chance during the life of the option to sell stock short at a higher price and then repurchase the shares at a lower cost. The holder of the call may sell and then buy the stock as many times as he wishes during this period without any risk of loss, so long as the sales price is above the exercise price.

Here is how-in-and-out trading against a call option might work: A 95-day call at 45 is acquired for a $300 premium. Then suppose stock rises to 50 and the trader sells stock short. If the price dips to 45, the short position could be covered by buying stock. Having fully absorbed the $300 premium cost, the trader at this point is $200 ahead (before commissions). Meanwhile, the call option is still effective and can be exercised should stock advance as originally anticipated.

PUTS

Some speculators like to buy put options, because puts are a superior substitute for selling stocks short. At a predetermined risk limited to the cost of the option, a put gets greater percentage

8

profit potential than by selling securities short. A put can be used for speculation on a small amount of capital, protection of a long position in a stock, in-and-out trading at limited risk or for achieving tax savings.

Although short selling is the traditional means of profiting from a drop in the price of a security, any profit from any short sale is always considered a short-term capital gain for tax purposes, no matter how long the short position remained open. A short sale, moreover, involves an extremely high degree of risk, since there is no limit to possible losses in such speculation.

In contrast with the unlimited risk of a short sale, the speculative use of a put option anticipates a profit from a drop in the price of the underlying stock at a predetermined risk limited to the premium paid for the option. Furthermore, a put is considered a capital asset so that a profit on a put may qualify as a long-term capital gain taxable at more favorable rates than any short sale. As a consequence, a put is the only means of converting a profit from a short position into a long-term capital gain.

To illustrate the speculative use of a put option, suppose a trader buys a 95-day put option on U.S. Steel stock at 40 for a $300 premium and then this option is exercised when the stock sells at 30. Such an account would show:

Sale of 100 U.S. Steel @ 40	$4,000
Purchase of 100 U.S. Steel @ 30	3,000
Gain on stock	1,000
Cost of put	300
Profit (before commissions)	$ 700

Had this trader sold stock short instead of purchasing put option, his profit would have amounted to $1,000 (less commissions) on a $4,000 sale, or a return of 25%. But by buying the put, his gain was $700 on the $300 cost of the option, or a return of

233%. However, if the price of the stock advanced, the option would have been allowed to expire unexercised and his loss would have been limited to the $300 cost of the put option.

This example illustrates the speculative use of a put for its leverage potential. Since an option premium is considerably less than the cost of the underlying stock, a given amount of cash can buy options covering a much larger quantity of shares than could be sold short. In this way, a put can benefit from a fall in the price of the related stock to a much greater extent than the outright short sale of the stock. However, if the stock does not decline during the life of the option, the entire investment in the option would be lost. Unlike a direct short sale of the shares, a put purchaser cannot wait for a drop in the price of the stock beyond the option's expiration date. In any event, a put does not become profitable until the stock falls in price by more than the amount of the premium paid for the option.

While the speculative use of an option as a superior substitute for selling stock short provides a highly leveraged short position, a put purchase may provide protection of a long position in a stock as a hedge against a possible decline in the price of the underlying stock. To illustrate, suppose an investor simultaneously buys stock and a 95-day put at 50 for a $300 premium. If the price of the stock falls precipitously, the put can be exercised in order to limit the loss to the cost of the premium paid for the option. On the other hand, should the price of the stock advance to over 53, the profit on the stock would offset the $300 option premium paid as insurance.

A put option makes possible in-and-out trading opportunities at limited risk, too. For instance, the holder of a put may buy and sell the stock as many times as he wishes during the life of the option, without any risk of loss, so long as the purchase price of the stock remains below the exercise price.

Here is how in-and-out trading against a put option might work: Suppose a trader simultaneously buys the stock and a 95-day put

10

option at 40 for a $300 premium and then sells the shares when the stock advances to 45. At this point, having fully absorbed the $300 premium cost, the trader is ahead $200. When the stock drops to 35, he buys the shares again, because he can put them to the option writer at 40. Should the stock rise to 45 again, he would sell stock. Meanwhile, the put option is still effective and can be exercised should stock fall as originally anticipated.

The only way to establish a long-term capital gain in a declining market is through the use of a put. Suppose, for example, a one-year put is purchased on U.S. Steel stock at 60 and then the stock drops to 40, so that the put is worth $2,000. Having been held the required length of time to qualify for tax purposes, the holder of this put can sell the option to establish a long-term profit taxable at the more favorable capital-gain rate. Put purchasing is the only way a long-term capital gain can be made on a short position in a stock, since a short sale is never eligible for long-term capital gains tax treatment.

STRADDLES

Put and call brokers and dealers prefer to buy straddle options, because the purchase of a straddle is generally less expensive than buying both the put and call separately. As a dual option combining one put and one call, the exercise of one contract before expiration does not void the remaining option. A straddle offers a security trader predetermined risk limited to the cost of this dual option and unlimited profit potential. A straddle option can be used for speculation on a small amount of capital, protection of a long or short position in the related stock or in-and-out trading at limited risk. Straddle strategy seeks very volatile vehicles, since such stocks are most risky and hence apt to fluctuate widely.

To illustrate, suppose a trader buys a one-year straddle option on a very volatile stock selling at 40 for a $800 premium. Then if the price advances to 50, stock should be sold short. If the price of the stock falls back to 40, the trader simply covers the short po-

11

sition by buying the shares in the market. At this point, having fully absorbed the premium cost, he is already ahead by $200 and he still owns the dual option. If the stock now drops to 30, the shares should be bought, because they can be put to the straddle writer at 40. Then if the stock price rises to 40, the sale of these shares would realize a $1,000 profit. Should stock subsequently move up to 50 again, the shares should be sold short, because the call could be exercised at 40.

OPTION WRITING

While an option is usually purchased for the purpose of either limiting a loss in an investment or speculating for unlimited profit potential, writers generally sell options for the purpose of increasing the return on their investment portfolio. Through the receipt of premium income, a greater return may be realized than on the stocks alone. In essence, an option writer is willing to acquire stock below the current market price or to sell shares above the current market price. If an option is not exercised, the option writer simply pockets the premium received.

Seldom do small investors or speculators sell options. Almost all option writing is done by substantial investors. Although the required capital to write a single option contract is not very large, a typical writer is prepared to supply contracts on numerous stocks in response to demand. These securities are either in his investment portfolio or on his list of eligible stocks which he is willing to purchase. As a consequence, writers are generally either individuals with large portfolios or financial institutions.

Most options are sold by individuals, although investment companies and insurance companies as well as pension funds have the large portfolios useful for successful option writing. Many institutional investors have been discouraged from participation in this field by seemingly legal deterrents and tax considerations, but government regulations are becoming more favorable towards option writing by both individuals and financial institutions.

12

An option writer is not generally too anxious to buy or sell stock at current market prices. By selling a put, however, the option writer may acquire stock at a lower price than the current market. By selling a call, an option writer may sell stock at a price higher than the current market. By selling straddles, an option writer is in a position to acquire stock below the current market price or sell shares above the current market price.

By selling puts, the premiums will reduce the cost of any stock acquired. By selling calls, the premiums will increase the profit on any shares sold. Generally, however, less than one-half of all put and call options are exercised, so that a writer can ordinarily expect to add premium income to the return on his investment portfolio, without actually being required to honor the obligations on the majority of put and call options written. In less than 1% of straddles written are both sides of the straddle exercised. When neither side or both sides of the straddle are exercised, his investment portfolio remains unchanged and the writer is ahead by the amount of the dual premium. This explains the eagerness of option writers to sell straddles rather than puts and calls alone.[4]

While the premium received from the sale of puts and calls is the key incentive for option writers to increase income and achieve larger capital gains, a run-up in the stock price might have yielded the covered call writer a larger gain than the premium income. In the case of a put, the price of the stock might drop so precipitously as to saddle the writer with a sizable loss. On an exercised put, nevertheless, the premium is used to reduce the cost of the security acquired. The proceeds from a call can be added to the contract price, thereby qualifying for a capital gain. Not the least of a writer's motivations is the fact that the majority of all options written are never exercised. What is more, the option writer receives the premiums in the from of cash paid in advance.

---

[4] U.S. Securities and Exchange Commission, Report on Put and Call Options, p. 52.

13

PUT WRITING

There is more than one way to buy stock. Most people purchase securities at prevailing market prices, but some sophisticated investors acquire stocks at prices below the current market by selling put options. Suppose an option writer were interested in buying 100 shares of U.S. Steel a few points below the current market price of 40 and thus sells a six-month put option for a $400 premium. Should the price of the stock decline, the put option would be exercised so that these shares would be delivered to the writer at the striking price of 40 and his account would show:

> Purchase of 100 U.S. Steel @ 40 .... $4,000
>
> less, put premium 400
>
> Net cost (before commissions) $3,600

Note that this option writer would be buying 100 shares of U.S. Steel common stock at a price actually 4 points or 10% below the market price of 40 at the time the put option was written. His cost, in effect, would be 36 for each share. On the other hand, had the price of the stock advanced, the put option would not have been exercised and the writer would have simply pocketed the $400 premium received from the sale of the put option. Since it is possible to sell two such six-month put options in a year, the annual rate of return would be some 22% on such a $3,600 investment.

A put writer is an investor who is willing to buy stocks below their current market prices. By selling puts, the option writer receives premiums which will reduce the cost of any such stock acquired. Although the price of a stock might drop so precipitously as to saddle the writer with a sizable loss, the cost of the acquired stock is surely less than a direct purchase without writing the put.

Actually, less than half of all put options are ever exercised.

14

Thus, the premiums received from the sale of the majority of all puts written are simply pocketed by option writers and this additional income raises the return on investment.

CALL WRITING

Just as there is more than one way to buy stock, there are also two ways to sell shares. While most people use the conventional method to sell securities at prevailing market prices, sophisticated option writers sell stock at prices above the current market by selling call options. Suppose an option writer were interested in disposing of 100 shares of U.S. Steel a few points above the current market price of 40 and sells a six-month call option for a $500 premium. Should the price of the stock decline, the call option would not be exercised and the writer would benefit by the $500 premium received from the sale of the call option. Since it is possible to sell two such six-month call options in a year, the annual rate of return would amount to nearly 29% on the $3,500 net investment in the stock ($4,000 less $500). Should the price of the shares rise instead of decline, the call option would be exercised and the writer would sell his 100 shares at the striking price of 40. His account would show:

Sale of 100 U.S. Steel @ 40 .... $4,000

Call Premium 500

Total proceeds (before commissions) $4,500

Note that this option writer would be selling 100 shares of U.S. Steel common stock at a price actually 5 points or some 12% above the market price of 40 at the time the call option was written. Through receipt of the premium income, the total return would be greater than through the sale of the stock alone. He will have received, in effect, 45 for each share. As a covered option

15

writer holding the underlying stock, however, he not only sacri-
ficed any opportunity to profit from a price increase exceeding the
amount of the premium, but retained the risk of loss had the price
of the stock declined below 35 (his reduced cost).

A covered call writer is an investor who is willing to sell stock
above the current market price. Through the sale of a call option,
the option writer receives a premium which will increase the
proceeds of any such shares sold should the price of the stock advance. On the other hand, if the price declines, the covered call
writer retains his shares and simply pockets the premium received.

NAKED WRITING

In contrast to the covered option writer holding the underlying
stock as protection against a price advance, the "naked" or uncovered call writer has no such position relating to the underlying
stock. The "naked" writer hopes to realize premium income from
option writing, without ownership of the underlying stock. If the
price of the stock does not rise above the striking price, the call
option will not be exercised and the uncovered writer will gain
the full amount of the premium. If the price of the stock rises,
however, the call will be exercised and the "naked" writer will be
required to purchase the stock at the higher current price to meet
the call. In effect, the "naked" call writer has sold short, with unlimited loss potential. The "naked" writer is thus clearly and completely exposed to dangerous risks, unlike the covered call writer
unaffected by the extent of a rise in the price of the underlying
stock. Since the uncovered call writer is not protected at all against
a rise in the price of the stock and is clearly and completely exposed to such risk of losses without any limit whatsoever, the
uncovered call writer is surely a "naked" writer.

Like a short seller, the "naked" or uncovered call writer generally expects a decline in the price of the related stock during the
life of the option. Should the price of the stock actually decline

16

or remain unchanged, the "naked" call writer simply pockets the premium. However, if the stock advances, the "naked" call writer is clearly vulnerable to the possibility of unlimited losses.

STRADDLE WRITING

Straddle writing can produce greater premium income than selling individual puts or calls. By the simultaneous sale of both a put and a call on the same stock, the straddle writer can in effect acquire shares below the current market price or sell shares above the market price.

Suppose a straddle writer were interested in either buying an additional 100 shares of U.S. Steel common stock several points below the current market price of 40, or selling shares several points above the market price. To accomplish this objective, he may sell a six-month straddle option for an $800 premium. Should the price of the stock decline, the put side of the straddle option would be exercised and 100 shares would be delivered to the writer at the striking price of 40. In such event, his account would show:

```
Purchase of 100 U.S. Steel @ 40 .......................... $4,000

Less, straddle premium ..........................................    800
                                                                 _____
Net cost (before commissions) ...........................  $3,200
```

Note that this option writer would in effect be buying 100 shares of U.S. Steel stock at a price equivalent to 8 points or 20% below the market price of 40 at the time the straddle option was written. On the other hand, if the price of stock advanced, the call side of the straddle would be exercised and the writer would sell his 100 shares at the striking price of 40. In such case, his account would show:

17

Sale of 100 U.S. Steel @ 40	$4,000
Straddle premium	800
Total proceeds (before commissions)	$4,800

In this event, the option writer would in effect be selling stock at a price equivalent to 8 points or 20% above the market price of 40 when the straddle option was written.

In infrequent instances, neither the call option nor the put option side of the straddle is exercised. This can occur if the market price of the stock at the expiration of the contract is close to the striking price. When this rare situation happens, the writer neither sells nor buys any shares of stock, but is ahead by the full amount of the straddle premium.

Since a straddle consists of both a put and a call option, the exercise of one does not void the other option. If both options are exercised during the life of the straddle contract so that the stock is both bought and sold, there is no net change in the writer's investment portfolio. Consequently, the option writer is ahead by the amount of the straddle premium (less commisions). This occurs in less than 1% of all straddles written.

In any event, a straddle writer engages in buying stocks below market prices, selling stocks above market prices, or adding premium income to the total return on his investment portfolio. Hence, it is in the nature of option writing to sell stocks after a rise and to accumulate shares when their prices are depressed—a sound investment procedure!

SPREAD WRITING

Occasionally, a spread option is written instead of a straddle. A spread is a variation of the straddle, in which the call price is usually above the market and the put price below the market. Compared to a straddle, as a rule, the premium paid by the option

18

buyer or received by the option writer is reduced by $50 for each point spread. The spread of 2 points, for example, reduces the premium by one point, or $100. For an option writer, the advantage of a spread is that it is less likely to be exercised, but he does receive a reduced premium.

Suppose that instead of writing a straddle (both the put and call at 40 for 6 months for $800), this option writer sells a put at 39 and a call at 41 (a 2 point spread) for a $700 premium. If the market price of the stock at the expiration of the contract is between 39 and 41, neither the put nor the call will be exercised and the spread writer will be ahead by the full amount of the $700 premium.

Some option writers prefer to sell straddles rather than spreads, because the immediate premium income received from the sale of a straddle option is larger. In the case of a straddle, however, at least one side of the option is normally exercised. This likelihood tends to boost brokerage commissions on straddles as against spreads.

The wider the spread between the put and call striking prices, the less likely either side of the spread option will be exercised. Suppose an option writer sells a put at 34 and a call at 46 (a 12 point spread) for a $200 premium. If the market price of the stock at the expiration of the contract is in the range between 34 and 46, neither the put nor the call will be exercised and the spread writer would be ahead by the full amount of the premium. In such a broad spread (15% of the market price in both directions), the empirical probability of either side of a 190-day straddle option on a typical stock being exercised is approximately 40%. Less than one-quarter of such calls or less than one-fifth of such puts will normally be exercised, so that the majority of these broad spreads are expected to expire without being exercised. On the other hand, the buyer of such a broad spread usually pays a relatively small premium for this type of option.

19

CHAPTER 2

Experience

Jacob wished to exercise his option when he completed his seven years labor as the premium paid for his call on the hand of Rachel, Laban's younger daughter. After the wedding feast that night, Laban brought his eldest daughter to Jacob and he slept with her. When morning came, he found dull-eyed Leah in his bed, but not beautiful Rachel. Jacob asked Laban, "Why have you deceived me?" Laban replied, "It is not right to give the younger sister in marriage before the elder. The younger shall be given you in return for a further seven years' work."[1]

Thus, Jacob acquired a second call option on Rachel's hand by paying an additional premium. After that call was exercised and the marriage finally consummated, the couple's first offspring was Joseph.[2] It was this same Joseph who later forecast the seven-year

[1] The Bible—Genesis 29.
[2] Genesis 30.

21

famine and planned the ever normal granary to stabilize the Egyptian economy.[3] In effect, his grandfather was the first option writer, his father the first option buyer, his mother the first call option, and Joseph the first dividend of an option contract.

The earliest successful speculator in call options on record was Thales, the first eminent Greek philosopher, also renowned as an astronomer and mathematician. According to Aristotle, Thales "knew by his skill in the stars while it was yet winter that there would be a great harvest of olives in the coming year; so, having a little money, he gave deposits for the use of all the olive-presses in Chios and Miletus, which he hired at a low price because no one bid against him. When the harvest-time came, and many were wanted all at once and all of a sudden, he let them out at any rate which he pleased, and made a quantity of money." In this way, Thales amassed his fortune by exercising call options.[4]

Early in the seventeenth century in Holland, both put and call options came into widespread use during the tulip-bulb boom. These options were employed for either hedging or speculation. For example, a tulip tradesman who contracted to deliver bulbs was assured of a sufficient supply at a predetermined price by buying call options. Similarly, a grower purchased put options to deliver tulips at a set price. At the same time, speculators used options to maximize their return from price fluctuations. As long as tulip prices soared, realized returns to call buyers and put writers rocketed. Finally, in 1636, the collapse of tulip prices and the end of the tulip-bulb craze destroyed that market. Hardest hit were put writers.

Throughout history, business options flourished. Phoenician merchants sold options on goods aboard their ships. In the United States, railroad pioneers employed options to acquire land on their routes. Virtually all oil and gas leases have contained option

---

[3] Genesis 41.

[4] The Works of Aristotle, vol. X Politics, J. A. Smith and W. D. Ross, ed. (London: Oxford University Press, 1921) p. 1259 a.

clauses. Bernard Baruch acquired options on mining and smelting companies for the Guggenheims who were expanding the American Smelting and Refining Company. The New York Yankees got Joe DiMaggio via a call option contract.[5]

Of course, not all business options are security options. How have options on securities fared?

SECURITY OPTIONS

Trading in security options made its formal debut in England late in the seventeenth century. There developed a well organized market in puts and calls on both bonds and stocks on the London Stock Exchange as well as on the provincial stock exchanges. As a matter of fact, the first specialized book on security options was published in London.[6]

Security option markets also developed in Holland, Belgium, Germany, Switzerland and France. While the London Stock Exchange had provided the first important security option market in the world, trading in puts and calls on the Paris Bourse became very sophisticated.

THE FRENCH CONNECTION

The rational theory of option pricing was initiated in 1900 by a French mathematician, Louis Bachelier. His ingenious option value formula was based on his discovery of the theory of Brownian motion five years ahead of Albert Einstein's classic paper on the Brownian motion of atoms.[8]

[5] Anthony M. Reinach, The Nature of Puts and Calls (New York: Bookmailer, 1961) Ch. V.

[6] Charles Castelli, The Theory of Options in Stocks and Shares (London: Mathieson, 1877).

[7] Louis Bachelier, Theory of Speculation (Paris: Gauthier-Villars, 1900) translated in The Random Character of Stock Market Prices, P. H. Cootner, ed. (Cambridge, Mass.: M.I.T. Press, 1964) pp. 17-78.

[8] Paul A. Samuelson, "Rational Theory of Warrant Pricing", Industrial Management Review, Spring 1965, pp. 13-32.

As the earliest scientific study of security options, Bachelier deduced an elaborate probability theory of speculative prices and then conducted an empirical investigation of the French government bond market, in order to test his mathematical theory explaining prices of various types of options including puts, calls, straddles and spreads. His empirical study showed that option prices corresponded closely to calculated expected values, based on theoretical or mathematical probabilities.

These results strongly suggested that option pricing is rational and that fluctuations in security prices are independent of all prior changes. This price independence, which indicates that prices cannot be forecast on the basis of past history, is the essence of the hypothesis now known as the random walk of stock prices.[9] If price fluctuations were positively correlated, options would be priced more expensively than predicted by Bachelier's theory. If changes in prices tended to reverse direction, options would be less costly. Since the random walk or Brownian motion indicates that serial or successive fluctuations are neither negatively nor positively correlated, actual option premiums proved to be in line with forecasts by Bachelier's theory of option values.

However, Bachelier's option value formula ignored the problem posed by the asymmetry of the distribution of security prices: Prices cannot fall below zero, but have no upper limit. This asymmetry problem actually justifies use of the "long-normal" distribution, dealing with changes in the logarithms of security prices rather than their arithmetic level. The factual existence of asymmetry in the distribution of stock prices helps explain why premiums are generally greater on call options than on put options.

Bachelier deduced the principle that "The value of a simple option must be proportional to the square root of time." This means, for example, that the value of a twelve-month option is normally twice as large as a three-month option, because the price

---

[9] Similar to the mathematical theory of Brownian motion describing a particle subject to random shocks.

of a stock over a twelve-month period will fluctuate twice as wide-ly as over a three-month period. Hence, the option premium in-creases in proportion to the square root of the contract's duration. A four-month option would cost twice as much as a one-month option, since the square root of 4 equals 2. Longer-term options, thus command greater premiums than short-term options, because stock prices are liable to wider dispersion over the long run.

Also deduced was the principle that "The premium of op-tions . . . is proportional . . . to the square of the coefficient of in-stability." For this reason, options on volatile stocks command greater premiums than on stable securities.

In his conclusion, Bachelier explained that he "compared the results of observation with those of theory . . . not to verify for-mulas established by mathematical methods, but only to show that the market unwittingly, obeys the law of probability."

AMERICAN EXPERIENCE

In the United States, puts and calls have been traded in the over-the-counter option market since the latter part of the eight-eenth century. The volume of trading in options has grown along with the volume of transactions in common stocks. In the face of their growing importance, however, there was no known scientific study or any empirical investigation of options in America until after the 1929 stock market debacle.

U.S. Senate Banking Committee hearings revealed that many of the financial abuses of the 1920's were somewhat or somehow related to the use or abuse of options. Many manipulative opera-tions were based on the granting of option to pools and syndicates. The U.S. Securities and Exchange Commission, therefore, was empowered by the Securities Exchange Act of 1934 to regulate op-tions along with other types of securities. Company options pri-vately offered in large blocks for manipulative purposes were cur-tailed by the anti-manipulative provisions of the Act, but so-called "legitimate" options publicly offered at a fixed premium on a competitive basis could be regulated by the Commission.[10]

Hence, regulation of security options by the U.S. Securities and Exchange Commission has not been chiefly concerned with stock options to officers and employees of corporations or with other private option agreements, but has concentrated on fully negotiable options publicly offered. Since 1937, regular reports on the volume of trading in puts and calls have been received from the Put and Call Brokers and Dealers Association. Since these statistical reports showed a very substantial increase in the volume of options, the Commission in 1959 authorized its staff to conduct a detailed study of stock options.

S. E. C. STUDY

By means of questionnaires to all member firms of the New York Stock Exchange and the Put and Call Brokers and Dealers Association as well as by supplemental information obtained through interviews, this Securities and Exchange Commission study yielded important data on the option market never before assembled.[11]

This major S. E. C. statiscal study covered all options sold or outstanding during the month of June 1959. Outstanding were options on a total of 3,735,000 shares of common stock. During that month, options on 630,850 shares were sold. Some 42% of all the options included in the study were exercised, comprising a bare 40% of the put options and 43% of the call options.

The public paid $1.5 million for call options on 381,000 shares, but recovered only 58% of their total investment in these options. In fact, a mere 18% of the call options earned a profit for their holders. In all, the purchase of calls resulted in a 42% average loss on investment.

---

[10] U.S. Senate, Stock Exchange Practices, Hearings before the Committee on Banking and Currency, 73rd Congress, 1st session, 1933, p. 7063.

[11] U.S. Securities and Exchange Commission, Report on Put and Call Options, August 1961.

These totals, though, fail to tell the whole story. The month of June 1959 may well have been a particularly poor time to buy calls, due to the drop in stock prices during the third quarter of that year. While most of the options were widely used for low-cost but unsuccessful speculation, the sophisticated investor could make other highly profitable uses of both puts and calls. To be sure, options may be bought as a hedge or insurance against a security position. Consider, for instance, the position of a speculator who buys a call as a hedge against his short position in a stock. If the price of the underlying stock declines and there is a profit on the short position, the failure to exercise the call option clearly cannot be cited as an instance of unsuccessful speculation. Similarly, consider the investor who purchases a put as a hedge against his ownership of stock, in order to obtain insurance against a drop in its market value. If the price of the shares rises, failure to put the stock surely cannot be cited as an example of unsuccessful investment anymore than the failure to collect on a term life insurance policy. Obviously, since you are still alive, was the premium paid on your life insurance policy really a poor investment? The payment of an option premium as a form of insurance is no more a "loss" than in the case of other insurance.

This S. E. C. study reported that the real motive in option writing is based on the expectation that the option will not be exercised. Less than one-half of all options are exercised, so that a writer has better than a 50-50 chance to add premium income on his portfolio, without being called upon to change his investment position. While the writer is not anxious to sell stock or add to his portfolio at current market prices, he would be willing to sell at a higher price or buy at a lower price. By writing a put or a call, the seller receives a premium which will reduce the cost of any stock acquired or increase the profit on any shares sold.

Writers, who are willing either to acquire shares below the current market price or to sell stock above the market price, may sell straddles. It is very unlikely that both sides of a straddle will be exercised and the writer can get a larger premium for a straddle than for a put or a call alone. If both sides of the straddle should be exercised, the writer's investment portfolio will remain unchanged and he will be ahead by the amount of the dual premium. Actually, both sides of the straddle are exercised in less than 1% of all straddles written.

But only 3% of the straddles written are sold as such to ultimate option buyers, who are chiefly interested in calls. Because of the greater demand for calls than puts and the clear preference by writers to sell straddles, the practice of converting options has developed so that about 80% of all puts written are converted into call options. While option conversion provides a riskless and profitable source of income for converters, only two dozen New York Stock Exchange member firms engage in this arbitrage activity.

The average premium received by writers of six-month call options was 12% of the value of the optioned stock, while buyers paid 14% average premiums. This spread, between the 14% paid by buyers and 12% received by writers, provided put and call brokers and dealers a typical 15% average gross profit ratio.

Writers of six-month calls on low-priced shares received premiums averaging 17% of the value of the optioned stock, while they got only 9% on high-priced shares. Option buyers pay considerably larger percentage premiums on low-priced stocks, because basically an option is purchased for the purpose of limiting the amount of loss on a security investment or speculation, while giving the holder unlimited profit potential. Thus, speculators with limited capital are especially attracted to options on low-priced shares.

Inasmuch as the loss on a call option is limited to the amount of the premium paid regardless of the extent of any drop in the price of the optioned stock and whereas the holder of a call stands to benefit most from the possibility of a very large gain in the price of the underlying stock, premiums paid for options on the most volatile securities tend to be the largest. In contrast, the writer's

28

profit is the greatest when the price of the stock remains unchanged. Consequently, percentage premiums on stable securities tend to be smaller than on volatile stocks. This S.E.C. finding that volatile stocks command much greater option premiums than stable securities supports Bachelier's principle that "The premium of options . . . is proportional . . . to the square of the coefficient of instability."

This S.E.C. study also clearly demonstrated that the percentage premium on options varies directly with the duration or length of the option. "The premium on a six-month option was equal to twice the premium on a 30-day option; it was one and a half times the premium on a 90-day option; and it was two-thirds of the premium on a one-year option."

This statistical evidence supports Bachelier's principle that "The value of a simple option must be proportional to the square root of time." For instance, applying Bachelier's probability value formula, a six-month option is worth 1.41 times as much as a three-month option, which in turn is worth 1.22 times a two-month option. The S.E.C. data showed that the premium on a six-month option actually averaged 1.46 times as much as a three-month option, which in turn averaged 1.23 times a two-month option. Clearly, these average results were remarkably close to their probability values, as indicated by Bachelier in 1900.

In retrospect, though the test period of June 1959 was not a good time to buy call options, it was an even poorer period to purchase puts. In the second half of 1959, as a matter of fact, the stock market price averages actually advanced on net balance. As a consequence, even fewer puts than calls were exercised. Whereas 43% of all call options were exercised, only 40% of the put options were exercised by their holders.

Of particular interest is the experience of option buyers of the 25 most popular stocks under option. While 47% of these call options were exercised, only 36% of the put options were exercised. Thus, buyers of the most popular puts fared much worse than buyers of popular call options.

In summary, some 58% of all puts and calls expired without being exercised. Moreover, any evidence of profitable buying of either puts or calls was clearly lacking.

MASSACHUSETTS INSTITUTE OF TECHNOLOGY

At the Massachusetts Institute of Technology, there have been a number of studies of security options involving both theoretical and empirical investigations. First, their studies utilized capital theory and the random-walk theory of security prices in model building to explain stock-option values. Second, their statistical studies sought to test the rationality of option dealing, by comparing average payoffs on option buying with the actual cost of options. Results of many of these empirical investigations at M.I.T. are presented here for critical review:[12]

KRUIZENGA

In a doctoral dissertation under the direction of Nobel Laureate Paul Samuelson, Richard J. Kruizenga used methods similar to Bachelier's to evaluate both put and call options. Covering almost a ten-year period from 1946 to 1956, Kruizenga analyzed hypothetical purchases of puts and calls on the basis of nominal premiums regularly reported to the U.S. Securities and Exchange Commission. The payoffs on an eight-stock average was compared with the cost of such options, to determine the profitability of the contracts. However, transaction costs were explicitly omitted from the computation of profitability, on the alleged but unsubstantiated ground that this omission tended to compensate for nominal quotes being higher than actual market premiums.[13]

---

[12] Much of this work plus related studies in *The Random Character of Stock Market Prices*, Paul H. Cootner, ed. (Cambridge, Mass.: M.I.T. Press, 1964).
[13] Richard J. Kruizenga, "Profit Returns from Purchasing Puts and Calls," *ibid.*, pp. 392-411.

His principal findings were that buying calls would have been profitable, but purchasing puts were clearly unprofitable. On average, call premiums were lower than their "actuarial values," in terms of changes in stock prices plus dividend payments. "Put premiums were very substantially larger than the actuarial values of puts."

The treatment of dividends in option contracts made calls significantly more valuable and puts much less valuable. If an over-the-counter call option is exercised, dividends during the life of the contract generally go to the call buyer. If a conventional put option is exercised, dividends go to the option writer. This difference in dividend treatment increased the actuarial value of calls by 24% and decreased the actuarial value of puts by 27%.

Kruizenga contended that his findings were contrary to the prevailing presumption that option buying is unprofitable and that returns to option writers are substantial. His most significant conclusion was "that on average option buyers could have made positive profits over a 10-year period." He added that "option writers would have shown losses when the results of their option writing were compared to their opportunities for gain by holding stock." His results showed that the buying of six-month calls would have realized an annual profit of 35% and that 90-day calls would have realized an annual profit of 9%. On an overall basis, the return on investment in calls came to some 24% per annum.

This ten-year period studied was far from representative, however, since it included the relatively extreme bull market period from 1953 to 1956. After omitting these last three years of the study, the results showed that six-month calls would have returned an average annual profit of only 1% and 90-day calls would have suffered an average loss of 10%—despite the fact that during these seven years the optioned stocks provided a return of more than 16% per annum. Thus, call buyers would have experienced large losses when the results of their option buying were compared to their opportunities for gain by holding the underlying stock. As a

31

matter of fact, any speculator in 1946 who had attempted to remain fully invested in these call options could not have possibly
survived for the next ten years, because he would have been bank-
rupt long before the great bull market began in 1953.

In clear contrast, purchasing put options was unprofitable in
both periods. Between 1946 and 1956, holders of these 90-day put
options would have realized an average loss of 72%. Even if the
exceptional 1953-1956 period were excluded, holders of put options would still have suffered a 67% loss on their option investment.

BONESS

Focusing on actual transactions during the 1957-1960 period,
James A. Boness found that buying of either put or call options
resulted in large losses, but that option writing utilizing certain
strategies could have realized net gains that exceeded the return
from direct investment in the underlying common stock.[14]

In the sample of 256 option purchases between July 1957 and
July 1960, the realized loss to buyers was 82% of the investment
per annum. In fact, buyers lost much more rapidly on short-term
options than on long-term options. The percentage losses on put
purchases were about three times as bad as on call buying.

In the sample of 234 options sold to dealers in the same period,
the average annual rate of return on naked option writing was
only 4%. These results, however, varied widely with the type of
option contract written. While the return on straddles was less
than 1% and calls suffered a 1% loss, put writing actually
achieved a positive 38% rate of return on investment.

If a more conservative strategy were utilized by writing covered calls and straddles, the average annual rate of return

[14] James A. Boness, "Some Evidence of the Profitability of Trading in Put and
Call Options" in The Random Character of Stock Market Prices, Paul H. Cootner,
ed. (Cambridge, Mass.: M.I.T. Press, 1964), pp. 475-496.

amounted to a mere 2%. The return on straddles was a negative 1% and on calls a 3% loss, in contrast with the positive return of 38% on put writing.

Boness concluded that option buyers must expect large losses and that "writers who are unwilling to administer a complicated decision rule . . . are unable to earn at a rate equal to the expectation of other investors in common stocks." He demonstrated how a complicated mixed strategy would give option writers an annual rate of return of 18% and more.

KATZ

Covering a sample of 851 option contracts written over a 21 month period from April 1960 to January 1962, Richard C. Katz found that 76 option writers had an average return on capital of less than 1%. While two-thirds of the writers made profits, most of them would have made a greater return had they invested their capital directly in their covering stock without writing any options.[15]

Using the same data compiled by Katz, a sample of 100 options covering the period from April 1960 to November 1961 was randomly drawn and then analyzed by Boness.[16] Utilizing the adventurous strategy of naked option writing, the annual average rate of return came to some 137%. While the sale of puts returned 79% on investment, the writing of both calls and straddles achieved returns exceeding 100%.

The conservative strategy of writing covered options showed an annual average rate of return on investment of nearly 28%. Call options, however, scored only a 7% return. Put writing achieved a 14% return. The highest average rate of return was some 37% on straddle writing.

---

15 Richard C. Katz, "The Profitability of Put and Call Option Writing," *Industrial Management Review*, Fall 1963, pp. 55-69.
16 Boness, pp. 493-496.

In a study of all options sold through a large brokerage firm during the years 1957-1960, Richard N. Rosett found that the holders of calls on ten of the most frequently optioned stocks (accounting for 20% of all options) lost 40% of their investment and that less than 43% of these options on 118,000 shares were exercised. In the case of the 25 most popular stocks involving some 218,000 shares under option, an even smaller percentage of call options was exercised.[17]

Rosett conjectured that call option buyers dislike variance in asset prices, but prefer high expected values and positive skewness of probability distributions. In other words, purchasers of call options are attracted by the asymmetrical distribution of stock prices, which provide a small chance for a very large gain against the high probability of a small loss. In Rosett's own words: "Thus large values of expected return are preferred to small, small values of variance are preferred to large, and right skewness is desirable."[18]

The preference for less variance by call buyers implies that the value of an option on a low variance or stable security may be overestimated and thus could be overpriced.

CALLS ON CONVERTIBLES

Covering the period from 1960 to 1967, Charles L. Hubbard and Terry Johnson conducted a simulated study of the practice of writing call options on stock, with the options hedged by the ownership of convertible bonds. Included in this selected sample were 16 such bonds bought on margin. Nominal premiums on six-month calls were chosen from advertisements by put and call dealers.[19]

[17] Richard N. Rosett, "Estimating the Utility of Wealth from Call Options Data" in *Risk Aversion and Portfolio Choice*, Donald Hester and James Tobin, ed. (New York: Wiley, 1967), pp. 154-169.

[18] *Ibid.*, pp. 164-165.

[19] Charles L. Hubbard and Terry Johnson, "Profits from Writing Calls with Convertible Bonds," *Financial Analysts Journal*, Nov.-Dec. 1969, pp. 78-89.

Hubbard and Johnson found that the annual rate of return from writing these call options would have been 60% during 1960-1965 and 20% during 1965-1967, when the lower returns resulted from "a combination of high margin requirements, rising interest rates and falling bond prices." They concluded that an overall rate of return close to 40% on writing of call options supported by convertible bonds is a "reasonable expectation."

PRINCETON UNIVERSITY

At the Financial Research Center of Princeton University, extensive computer experiments have been conducted to explore the implications of various strategies available to investors and to assess the uefulness of the role that option buying or writing might play in optimal investment strategies. Results of these Princeton faculty studies have become available in various ways:

MALKIEL AND QUANDT

Performing some 1,056 computer experiments at the Financial Research Center of Princeton University, Burton G. Malkiel and Richard E. Qaundt employed two techniques to assess the role of option buying and writing in order to determine optimal investment strategies.[20]

First, they investigated how an investor would have fared had he engaged in some sixteen strategies during the 1960-1964 period, by comparing the returns from using options, or holding a common stock portfolio or Treasury Bills. It was assumed that an investor dealt in stocks selling between $45 and $55 per share on the New York Stock Exchange on the first of January in each of the five years. Then similar experiments were repeated for put purchases and for various option writing strategies, enabling payoff comparisons.

---

[20] Burton G. Malkiel and Richard E. Quandt, *Strategies and Rational Decisions in the Securities Options Market* (Cambridge, Mass.: M.I.T. Press, 1969).

The second technique employed several methods of game theory as well as decision theory by simulating strategy for various attitudes toward risk taking and different tax status. Both types of experiments led to similar results.

This Princeton study found that option writing was a better strategy than option buying. The results clearly showed that on average option buyers lost heavily, while many writing strategies brought larger profits and involved less risk than ownership of diversified portfolios of common stock.

The effect of buying six-month call options was a 37% average loss on investment, or a negative rate of return of 73% per annum. Put purchases resulted in a 35% loss on investment, equal to a negative rate of return of 70% per annum. Straddle buying incurred a 36% loss on investment, or a negative annual return of 72%. In the face of these substantial losses suffered by option buyers, Malkiel and Quandt said: "Option buying could be justified only by investors who expected large price changes on particular stocks and/or who derived benefit from the leverage afforded by option buying and who were not averse to the attendant risks."[21]

The optimal strategy was "naked" or uncovered straddle writing, which would have produced an average gain of over 14% on investment, or an annual rate of return of 28%. Covered straddle writing would have yielded an average annual gain of only 7%. While "naked" straddle writing is more exposed to the risk of rising stock prices, the covered straddle writer is subjected to double jeopardy from a declining market. Falling prices will cause a dual loss: one on the long position in the stock and the second loss on the put position.

Malkiel and Quandt, nevertheless concluded that a combination of stock buying and straddle writing was the most favored investment strategy for conservative institutional investors, espe-

---

[21] Burton G. Malkiel, "Trading in Options: What Are the Best Strategies?" *Commercial and Financial Chronicle*, Dec. 14, 1972, pp. 1 and 12.

cially those that are tax-exempt. Writing options against their portfolio would improve their investment returns substantially.

The empirical work of these authors disclosed that premium percentages on both calls and straddles are directly correlated to the past volatility of the underlying stock prices and to the turn-over ratio of shares traded to shares outstanding, but inversely correlated to the number of shares outstanding and the price of the stock. It was also discovered that the expected long-term growth rate for earnings of underlying stock (a proxy for ex-pected price appreciation) varied directly with percentage pre-miums on call options, but not on straddles. Although a higher expected growth rate could increase the ratio of the option pre-mium to the market price of the stock in the call position, growth could not enhance the value of the put side of the straddle.

For both calls and straddles, the volatility variable was the most significant factor explaining the variance in percentage premiums. The potential loss to the option buyer is limited to the premium paid, no matter how much the price of the underlying stock fluc-tuates. Therefore, the value of an option is clearly and directly related to the expected variance of the underlying shares.

Percentage premiums vary inversely with the price of the op-tioned stock, because presumably options are bought for the pur-pose of speculating on a minimum amount of capital and thus risk as little as possible. Since options on high priced shares will not enhance their potential return, option buyers favor low priced stocks.

This simulated study by Malkiel and Quandt may be criticized on two grounds: Their analysis was based on nominal quotations and not on actual option premiums. Secondly, the time covered by the study was far from a typical period. If an investor simply owned the underlying shares for the first half of each year during 1960-1964, the annual rate of return on investment in this un-usual period would have been less than one-half of 1%.

37

A more recent study at the Financial Research Center at Princeton University utilized the July 1963 to January 1965 period and included the ten stocks reported weekly by the Put and Call Brokers and Dealers Association as a sample of actively traded options. Again, the average returns on investment for some sixteen strategies were compared. The results were remarkably similar to the original Princeton University experiments.[22]

Option buying generally provided large losses, while option writing made moderate gains. Writing of options against a long position in a stock produced larger returns than a buy and hold strategy, though this entailed little or no added risk. "Naked" option writing produced large returns, but was exposed to much greater risk than any other strategy except option buying.

The largest profits were scored by six-month "naked" straddle writing, which would have produced an average gain of nearly 43% on investment, or an annual rate of return of some 85%. Covered straddle writing would have yielded an average gain of 10% on investment in six-month options, equal to an annual rate of return of 20%.

In the writing of three-month options, puts recorded the largest profits by producing an average gain of more than 12%, or an annual rate of return of almost 50%. On six-month options, put writing yielded nearly 24% on investment, or an annual rate of return of some 48%.

In contrast, the largest losses were incurred by put buyers. They would have suffered average losses exceeding 66% of their investment in six-month options and 64% in three-month options. Similarly, call buyers would have incurred average losses of 40% on investment in six-month options and 30% in three-month options.

---

[22] *Ibid.*

UNIVERSITY OF CHICAGO

At the University of Chicago, Merton H. Miller conducted a simulated study of buying and selling call options based on actual annual rates of return on common stock over the forty-year period 1926-1965. His study, however, ignored transaction costs and was calculated on a range of hypothetical premium percentages.[23]

If option premiums paid had averaged 24.4%, call buyers would have incurred a net loss equal to 4% of the value of the underlying stock, or 16% of the average investment in options. In clear contrast, "naked" or uncovered call writers would have received an average return of 4% of the value of the underlying stock, equal to 16% of their average investment in options. Covered call writers would have gained 18% on the value of their portfolio. Of this total return on investment, 14% would have been earned from the portfolio investment in shares alone, but only 4% from call writing.

Miller concluded that "when brokerage expense is taken into account, the aggregate losses from the losing strategies must have exceeded the aggregate gains from the seemingly profitable ones."[24] His results clearly demonstrated that call buying is generally unprofitable, but cast doubt on the profitability of call option writing. His simulated study was limited to call options and thus failed to investigate the results of all other possible option strategies.

BLACK AND SCHOLES

Fischer Black and Myron Scholes of the University of Chicago investigated the actual experience of option writing based on all contracts negotiated for customers by an option broker in the period from May 1966 to July 1969. In this empirical study were

[23] Merton H. Miller, "The Effects of an Improved Option Market on the Costs of Debt and Equity Capital," in Robert R. Nathan Associates, *Public Policy Aspects of a Futures-Type Market in Options on Securities,* vol. 2, pp. 35-51.
[24] *Ibid.,* p. 45.

six-month options on 545 securities covering 2,039 call contracts and 3,052 straddles involving more than a half million shares of optioned stock, for the purpose of testing a theoretical valuation formula for options.[25]

These empirical tests of the valuation formula applied to the call option data indicated that option writers receive premiums as predicted by the valuation formula, but that option buyers pay premiums that are consistently larger than their values. All of the large transaction costs in trading option were "effectively paid by option buyers."[26]

Black and Scholes also found that the excess of the premium paid by option buyers over the predicted formula value is larger on low-risk stocks than on high-risk stocks. The effect of differences in variance rate on option values appears to be understimated in premium prices. Thus, premiums paid on low variance securities tend to be too high and premiums on high variance securities tend to be too low.

During this strong "bull" market period, the average return on investment for covered call writers was hardly more than 6%, while the average return for investors in the underlying stock was nearly 10% and the average return to option buyers was 8%. Thus, outright investment in the underlying stocks showed better performance results than both call option buying and covered call option writing. Neither option buyers nor sellers fared as well as outright stock investment in that period, because transaction costs in over-the-counter option dealing were so great.[27]

---

[25] Fischer Black and Myron Scholes, "The Valuation of Option Contracts and a Test of Market Efficiency," *Journal of Finance*, May 1972, pp. 399-417.

[26] Fischer Black and Myron Scholes, "The Pricing of Options and Corporate Liabilities," *Journal of Political Economy*, May-June 1973, pp. 637-653.

[27] Myron Scholes, "Rational Option Pricing and Price Movements on the CBOE," in *Review of Initial Trading Experience at the Chicago Board of Options Exchange*, Robert R. Nathan Associates (Chicago Board of Options Exchange, Dec. 1974), Appendix B.

TENTATIVE CONCLUSION

Since no single strategy is best for all possible purposes, any general conclusion regarding the profitability of either buying or selling options has limited validity. The actuarial value of an option is dependent not only upon the probability distribution of the price of the underlying stock, but also on the strategy selected. The rate of return on either buying or writing options, in fact, clearly varies with the type of option contract as well as with the strategy and tactics employed.

CHAPTER 3

Simulated Strategy Study

The general lack of agreement among the various statistical studies of the experience of buyers and sellers of security options does not instill complete confidence in their results. Unfortunately, the scope of most of such empirical studies seems to be limited to testing whether buying or writing of options is profitable, without clearly distinguishing different results contingent upon the type of option or strategy utilized. Actually, the rate of return on investment in options depends not only on the actuarial value of the particular option contract, but also on the selected strategy employing different types of option contracts.

The author's own simulated study scrutinizes separately several strategies utilizing different types of option contracts. These actuarial calculations are based on the actual annual average rates of return on investment in common stocks in the forty-eight year period 1926-1973,[1] estimated transaction costs reflecting brokerage

---

[1] Lawrence Fisher and James H. Lorie, "Rates of Return on Investment in Common Stock: The Year-by-Year Record, 1926-1965," *Journal of Business,* July 1968, pp. 291-316 and also Standard & Poor's Security Price Index Record for 1966-1973.

commission rates effective in January 1975, and average premiums on six-month option contracts.[2]

CALL BUYING

Table I, for instance, displays the actuarial calculations of the average results of hypothetical purchases of two typical six-month call options on all common stocks listed on the New York Stock Exchange every year during the 1926-1973 period. In 19 of these 48 years (40% of the period), the stock market averages actually declined, so that the call options would have expired unexercised and the entire investment in these options would have been lost. In the other 29 years (60% of the time), the market averages advanced, so that the gross return on the exercise of calls would have amounted to some 31.7% of the initial value of the optioned stock. Averaging this return in the profitable years with the zero return in the losing years results in a weighted average gross return of 19% on the initial value of the underlying shares. Since the premiums paid for two typical six-month call options each year would have totaled 28%, buyers would have had an average loss of 9%. After taking into account brokerage commissions paid on the calls exercised (60% of the total options), the average net return from buying call options would have amounted to a net loss of 11.4% on the initial value of the optioned stock (or nearly 41% of the investment in call options).

As an appraisal of their profitability or more accurately their negative profitability, this 41% average loss on investment by buyers of call options often encounters a conceptual objection. It is alleged that call options may be bought as a hedge or insurance against a security position and not necessarily as a vehicle for speculation on the optioned stock. If call options are really used for hedging or insurance purposes, then their utility or usefulness

---

[2] U.S. Securities and Exchange Commission, Report on Put and Call Options, August 1961.

44

could be tested in terms of the relationship between the risk incurred and the premium paid for such insurance rather than in terms
of their profitability to buyers of options.

TABLE I

Returns to Call Option Buyers
(as % of initial share price)

1926—1973

(1) Average gross return on exercise of calls in years of market decline 0

(2) Average gross return on exercise of calls in years of market rise 31.7

(3) Weighted average gross return .4 x (1) + .6 x (2) 19.0

(4) Average premiums paid for call options 28.0

(5) Average return from buying calls (3) —(4) ....—9.0

(6) Brokerage commissions paid .6 x 4 % 2.4

(7) Average net return from buying calls (5) —(6) ....—11.4

In fact, call option buying has a hedging effect only when combined with a short position. In order to protect or insure an existing security position, a call must be acquired as a hedge against a
short position in the underlying stock. In the event of arise in the
market price, the short seller can exercise the call to cover the
short position without a loss on the stock. In the event of a decline,
the short position is covered by buying the stock in the open
market to realize the profit and refraining from exercising the call.
In this way, an option may be used as insurance against a loss on
a short sale.

Unless you intend to commit arson when you insure your home
against fire, you do not aim to profit from the insurance. Similarly,
the cost of an option as a hedge against a loss on a short sale represents insurance. Thus, an expired or lapsed call does not necessarily mean that the option holder suffered a loss. As a matter of

45

fact, an option holder refrains from exercising a call when his short position in the related stock is profitable. Payment of a premium as a form of insurance is no more a "loss" than in the case of other insurance.

If options were purchased primarily as a hedge or insurance, fewer calls than puts would be bought since short positions are much smaller than long positions. Actually, however, call purchases are rather consistently larger than put purchases, for only a relatively small number of options are really bought for insurance or hedging purposes. When an option holder exercises a call, the acquired stock is usually resold immediately. Because most options are bought basically for speculation on a small amount of capital, more relevant than risk insurance is the rate of return on investment in options.[3]

This 41% average loss on investment by buyers of call options in the forty-eight year period 1926-1973 indicated in this study is exactly the same result as the 41% average loss found in the U.S. Securities and Exchange Commission Report on Put and Call Options. Moreover, it also virtually substantiates the 40% average loss on investment by buyers of call options reported by both Rosett[4] and Malkiel.[5] The preponderance of evidence surely tends to indicate clearly and convincingly that typical purchases of call options for speculative purposes are not generally profitable.

NAKED CALL WRITING

Table II shows the actuarial calculations of the average results of typical sales of "naked" or uncovered call options on all common stocks listed on the New York Stock Exchange during the 1926-73 period. In 19 of these 48 years (40% of the time), the

---

[3] *Ibid.*, pp. 2, 5, 14, 76, 77.

[4] Richard N. Rosett, "Estimating the Utility of Wealth from Call Options Data" in *Risk Aversion and Portfolio Choice,* Donald Hester and James Tobin, ed. (New York: Wiley, 1967), pp. 154-169.

[5] Burton G. Malkiel, "Put and Call Options," *Wall Street Transcript,* October 26, 1972, pp. 30,810-30,812.

stock market averages declined, so that the call options would have expired unexercised and the writers would have gained the entire premiums received. In the other 29 years (60% of the period) when the market advanced, the calls would have obligated the writers to deliver stock selling at an average 31.7% higher than the initial striking price. Averaging this loss with the zero loss in the other years results in a weighted average loss of 19%. Since the premiums received totaled 24%, the writers would have had a gross return of 5%. After deducting brokerage commissions paid on the calls exercised (60% of the total), the average net return from writing "naked" or uncovered call options would have amounted to a mere 2.6% of the initial value of the optioned shares (or less than 11% of the premiums received).

Table II

Returns to Naked Call Writers
(as % of initial share price)

1926—1973

(1) Average loss on exercise of calls in years of market decline 0

(2) Average loss on exercise of calls in years of market rise 31.7

(3) Weighted average loss .4 x (1) + .6 x (2) 19.0

(4) Average premiums received 24.0

(5) Average return from writing calls (4) —(3) 5.0

(6) Brokerage commissions paid .6 x 4% 2.4

(7) Average net return from writing naked calls (5) —(6) 2.6

It is noteworthy that the total transaction costs in writing "naked" or uncovered calls are far from insignificant. Brokerage commissions on the exercise of calls can amount to some 10% of the total premiums received, or nearly half of the average gross return from writing "naked" call options.

47

This 2.6% annual rate of return on investment in "naked" or uncovered call option writing was significantly below the opportunity cost of available alternatives of investing directly in common stock or even buying U.S. Government bonds. In any event, there is no preponderance of evidence to clearly indicate that the sale of "naked" or uncovered call options is sufficiently profitable to option writers.

As a matter of fact, "naked" or uncovered call option writing is much riskier than investing directly in common stocks. The "naked" call writer, in effect, engages in short selling with the delivery date entirely out of his hands, so that there is no theoretical limit to his potential loss unless he can engage in closing purchase transactions.

Since a "naked" call exposes the option writer to unlimited risk as well as an inadequate or unsatisfactory return on investment, the sale of uncovered or "naked" calls does not surely seem attractive to option writers.

COVERED CALL WRITING

An option writer can hedge the sale of a call against a rise in the market price of the underlying stock by buying or owning the optioned stock. Unlike the "naked" call writer, the covered call writer is unaffected by the extent to which the price of the underlying stock rises. Although the covered call writer loses from downward price movements, no net loss is incurred unless the price of the stock falls by an amount exceeding the option premium.

Table III displays the picture of the actuarial calculations of the average results of typical sales of covered call options on all common stocks listed on the New York Stock Exchange during the 1926-1973 period. In those 29 years when the market rose, the return on the covering shares exactly offset any computed loss on the exercise of calls, so that the gains to writers would have been the full amount of the premiums received. In the 19 years when the market declined, the premium income was reduced by the loss

48

on the covering shares. After deducting brokerage commissions paid on the calls exercised by option holders, the average net return from writing covered call options would have amounted to 15.8% of the initial value of the optioned stock (or nearly 66% of the premiums received).

Not only does covered call option writing generally provide a high rate of return on investment, but it is also safer or less risky than investment in a portfolio of common stocks alone. When market prices decline, the premium income reduces the loss on the covering shares in the optioned portfolio. In contrast, the value of a widely diversified portfolio of common stocks swings with the market averages.

In addition to the investment return on a common stock portfolio, the covered call writer receives substantial option premiums. Hence, the total return on an optioned portfolio is generally greater than investment in that portfolio alone.

TABLE III

Returns to Covered Call Writers
(as % of initial share price)
1926—1973

(1) Average loss on exercise of calls in years of market rise 31.7

(2) Average return on covering share in years of market rise 31.7

(3) Average return in years of market rise (2) —(1) 0

(4) Average loss on exercise of calls in years of market decline 0

(5) Average loss on covering share in years of market decline 14.4

(6) Weighted average loss .4 x (5) + .6 x (3) 5.8

(7) Average premiums received 24.0

(8) Average return from writing covered calls (7) —(6) 18.2

(9) Brokerage commissions paid .6 x 4% 2.4

(10) Average net reurn from writing covered calls (8) —(9) 15.8

49

PUT PURCHASES

Unlike calls, it is often claimed that puts are purchased primarily for hedging and hence "the profitability of direct speculation in puts is of somewhat less interest."[6] This viewpoint may be justified on the grounds that: "Buyers of insurance pay more for insurance than its actuarial value, and option buyers would be expected similarly to pay more for options than on average they are worth."[7]

A put purchase has a hedging effect only when combined with a long position in the underlying stock. In the event of a decline in the market price, the option holder can exercise the put by delivering the shares to the option writer without incurring a loss on the stock. In the event of a rise in the price, the option holder realizes a profit on the optioned stock and refrains from exercising the put. Thus, it does not necessarily mean that the option holder has suffered a loss if a put expires unexercised. Where a put is purchased for the purpose of limiting the risk involved in owning the underlying stock, payment of the premium as a form of insurance is no more a "loss" than in the case of other insurance.

If options were purchased primarily as a hedge or insurance, many more puts than calls would be bought, since long positions are much larger than short positions. Actually, however, call purchases are consistently larger than put purchases, so that only a relatively small number of options are really bought for hedging or insurance purposes.[8] Since most options are bought basically for speculation on a small amount of capital rather than for hedging, more relevant than risk insurance is the computation of the rate of return on investment.

---

[6] Richard A. Brealey, Security Prices in a Competitive Market (Cambridge, Mass.: M.I.T. Press, 1971), p. 168.

[7] Richard J. Kruizenga, "Profit Returns from Purchasing Puts and Calls" in The Random Character of Stock Market Prices, Paul H. Cootner, ed. (Cambridge, Mass.: M.I.T. Press, 1964), p. 392.

[8] U.S. Securities and Exchange Commission, ibid.

Table IV

Returns to Put Option Buyers
(as % of initial share price)

1926—1973

(1) Average gross return on exercise of puts in years of market rise 0

(2) Average gross return on exercise of puts in years of market decline 14.4

(3) Weighted average gross return .6 x (1) + .4 x (2) 5.8

(4) Average premiums paid for put options 22.0

(5) Average return from buying puts (3) —(4) .... —16.2

(6) Brokerage commissions paid .4 x 4% 1.6

(7) Average net return from buying puts (5) —(6) .... —17.8

In table IV is the picture of the actuarial calculations of the average results of typical purchases of put options on all common stocks listed on the New York Stock Exchange during the 1926‑1973 period. In the 29 years when the market rose, the put options would have been allowed to expire unexercised, so that the entire investment in these options would have been lost. In the other 19 years when the market declined, the gross return on the exercise of the puts would have amounted to 14.4%. Averaging this return with the zero return in the losing years results in a weighted aver‑ age gross return of 5.8%. Since the premiums paid for put options totaled 22%, the buyers would have had a 16.2% loss. After de‑ ducting brokerage commissions paid on the puts exercised (40% of the total options), the average net return from purchasing put options would have amounted to a net loss equal to 17.8% on the initial value of the optioned stock (or nearly 81% of the invest‑ ment in put options).

The 81% average loss on investment by buyers of put options in the forty‑eight year period 1926‑1973 clearly demonstrates that put purchases are generally unprofitable. In fact, no known em‑

51

pirical study surely shows that put option buying is profitable. Furthermore, put purchases incur generally greater losses than even call buying.

Table V

Returns to Put Writers
(as % of initial share price)

1926—1973

(1) Average gross loss on exercise of puts in years of market rise 0

(2) Average gross loss on exercise of puts in years of market decline 14.4

(3) Weighted average gross loss .6 x (1) + .4 x (2) 5.8

(4) Average premiums received 18.0

(5) Average return from writing puts (4) —(3) 12.2

(6) Brokerage commissions paid .4 x 4% 1.6

(7) Average net return from writing puts (5) —(6) 10.6

PUT WRITING

Writing a put option and selling short is not a common strategy, although an option writer could hedge the sale of a put against a drop in the market price by a short sale of the optioned shares. While the short position ensures that the writer will purchase put stock and so protects the endorser of the option, it does not leave the writer in a riskless position in the event of a rise in the market price of the stock. Then the option would not be exercised by the put holder and the writer would be required to cover his short position on unfavorable terms. Thus, the so-called covered put writer in reality is not hedged, but is completely exposed to the risk of an unlimited rise in the price of the optioned shares. For this reason, put writers are not commonly covered by short sales and tend to engage in clearly "naked" put selling. Hence, writing a put and selling short is not a common strategy.

52

Unlike the unlimited risk exposure of the so-called covered put writer, the risk to a "naked" put writer is clearly limited to no more than the price of the optioned stock (less the amount of the premium received). As a matter of fact, the risk position of the so-called "naked" or uncovered put writer is practically the equivalent of a covered call writer who has hedged the sale of a call by buying or holding the underlying stock.

Table V shows the actuarial calculations of the average results of typical sales of "naked" or uncovered put options on all common stocks listed on the New York Stock Exchange in the forty-eight year period 1926-1973. In the 29 years when the stock market averages advanced, the put options would have been allowed to expire unexercised, so that the writers would have gained the entire premiums received. In the 19 years when the market declined, the puts would have required the writers to buy stock selling at an average of 14.4% below the initial striking price. Averaging this loss with the zero loss results in a weighted average gross loss of 5.8% Since premiums received totaled 18%, the writers would have had a gross return of 12.2%. After deducting brokerage commissions on the puts exercised (40% of the total options), the average net return from writing put options would have amounted to 10.6% on the initial value of the optioned stock (or almost 59% of the premiums received).

This 10.6% annual rate of return on investment in "naked" or uncovered put writing in the forty-eight year period 1926-1973 indicates that the sale of puts is generally profitable to the option writer. In fact, there is no known empirical study surely showing put writing to be unprofitable.

The computation of this 10.6% average rate of return on investment in put writing is based on the most conservative assumption that puts were written against 100% cash margin, while the minimum New York Stock Exchange margin requirement on the sale of put options is now 50%. On the basis of this minimum margin requirement, the annual rate of return on investment in put writing could thus come to some 21%. This result tends to support the 48% annual rate of return on "naked" put sales reported by Malkiel when the minimum margin requirement was only 25%.[9]

TABLE VI

Returns to Covered Straddle Writers

(as % of initial share price)

1926—1973

(1) Average loss on exercise of calls in years of market rise 31.7

(2) Average return on covering share in years of market rise 31.7
(8) Average loss on exercise of puts in years of market fall 14.4

(3) Weighted average loss on calls in years of market rise (2) —(1) 0

(4) Average loss on exercise of calls in years of market decline 0

(5) Average loss on covering share in years of market decline 14.4

(6) Weighted average loss on calls .6 x (4) + .4 x (5) 5.8

(7) Average loss on exercise of puts in years of market rise 0

(9) Weighted average loss on puts .6 x (7) + .4 x (8) 5.8

(10) Gross loss on calls and puts (6) + (9) 11.6

(11) Average premiums received 40.0

(12) Average return from writing straddles (11) —(10) 28.4

(13) Brokerage commissions paid 4.0

(14) Average net return from writing covered straddles (12) —(13) 24.4

STRADDLE WRITING

Table VI displays the actuarial calculations of the average results of covered straddle writing against an investment portfolio of all common stocks listed on the New York Stock Exchange in

---

[9] Malkiel, *ibid.*

54

the forty-eight year period 1926-1973. When the market rose, any loss on the exercise of calls was exactly offset by the return on the covering shares, so that the gain to the writers would have been the full premiums received. When the market declined, the premium income was reduced by the losses on the covering shares and on the exercise of puts requiring the writers to buy stock selling below the initial striking price. Deducting this 11.6% gross loss from the 40% total premiums received would have given a 28.4% return. After deducting brokerage commissions paid on the options exercised, the average net return from writing covered straddles would have amounted to 24.4% of the initial value of the optioned stock (or 61% of the premiums received).

This 24.4% annual rate of return on investment in covered straddle writing in the forty-eight year period 1926-1973 clearly indicates that the sale of straddle options against a diversified portfolio of common stock is generally profitable to option writers. This combination of holding a security portfolio and writing straddles against the long positions tends to produce substantially larger returns on investment than a buy and hold strategy, though this entails little or no added risk.

CBOE CALLS

Unlike traditional options traded in the over-the-counter market, the exercise or striking price of a Chicago Board Option is not adjusted for ordinary cash dividends paid on the underlying stock during the life of the option. This retention of the dividend may provide a Chicago Board Option writer with an added return.

Total transaction costs are generally smaller on the Chicago Board Options Exchange than in over-the-counter option trading for both option buyers and writers. The continuous auction market provided by a national securities exchange narrows the spread between what option buyers pay and what writers receive. Since a Chicago Board Option may be liquidated by a closing transaction

55

without either buying or selling the underlying stock, total transaction costs are reduced substantially. Brokerage commissions are computed on the price of a Chicago Option and not on the value of the related shares.

Table VII shows the actuarial calculations of the average results of hypothetical purchases of call options on all common stocks listed on the New York Stock Exchange every year during the 1926-73 period, assuming the existence of Chicago Board Option contract terms. In 19 of these 48 years (40% of the period) the stock market declined, so that these call options would expire unexercised and the entire investment in these options would have been lost. In the other 29 years (60% of the time), the market advanced, so that the gross return on the exercise of these calls would have amounted to 27% of the initial value of the optioned stock. Averaging this return in the profitable years with the zero return in the losing years results in a weighted average gross return of 16.2% on the initial value of the underlying stock. Since the premiums paid for the call options each year would have totaled

TABLE VII

Returns to Call Option Buyers on the
Chicago Board Options Exchange
(as % of initial share price)

1926—1973

(1) Average gross return on exercise of calls in years of market decline 0

(2) Average gross return on exercise of calls in years of market rise 27.0

(3) Weighted average gross return .4 x (1) + .6 x (2) 16.2

(4) Average premiums paid for call options 20.0

(5) Average return from buying call (3) —(4) .... —3.8

(6) Brokerage commissions paid 3.0

(7) Average net return from buying calls (5) —(6) .... —6.8

56

20%, buyers would have had an average loss of 3.8%. After taking into account brokerage commissions paid on the options, the average net return from buying Chicago Board Options would have amounted to a net loss of 6.8% on the initial value of the optioned stock (or 34% of the investment in call options).

The average gross return on exercised calls would have been 4.7% less on Chicago Board Options than on over-the-counter options, because the writer of a CBOE call retains the dividends paid during the life of the option. On the other hand, premiums paid for Chicago Board Options are substantially smaller than for over-the-counter options. The substantial spread between what the purchaser pays and what the writer receives, representing the 15% average mark-up by over-the-counter option dealers, does not exist on the Chicago Board Options Exchange.

The average net loss of 6.8% on buying CBOE options compares with the 11.4% net loss on the purchase of call options in the over-the-counter market. The improved results reflect the substantially smaller premiums paid for Chicago Board Options.

NAKED CBOE CALL WRITING

Table VIII displays the actuarial calculations of the average results of typical sales of "naked" or uncovered call options on all common stocks listed on the New York Stock Exchange during the 1926-73 period, assuming Chicago Board Option contract terms. In 19 of these 48 years (40% of the time), the stock market averages declined, so that these call options would have expired unexercised and the writers would have gained the entire premiums received. In the other 29 years (60% of the period) when the market advanced, the calls obligated the writers to deliver stock selling at an average 27% higher than the initial striking price. Averaging this loss with the zero loss in the other years results in a weighted average loss of 16.2%. Since the premiums received totaled 20%, the writers would have had a gross return of 3.8%. After deducting brokerage commissions paid on the options, the average net return from writing "naked" or uncovered CBOE call options would have amounted to less than 1% of the initial value of the optioned shares (or 4% of the premiums received).

Table VIII

Returns to Naked Call Writers on the Chicago Board Options Exchange
(as % of initial share price)

1926—1973

(1) Average loss on exercise of calls in years of market decline 0

(2) Average loss on calls in years of market rise 27.0

(3) Weighted average loss .4 × (1) + .6 × (2) 16.2

(4) Average premiums received 20.0

(5) Average return from writing calls (4) —(3) 3.8

(6) Brokerage commissions paid 3.0

(7) Average net return from writing naked calls (5) —(6) 0.8

This relatively small return on investment in "naked" or uncovered call option writing on the Chicago Board Options Exchange is not significantly different from the computed rate of return on writing "naked" call options in the over-the-counter market. In both cases, like students streaking, "naked" call writing is not clearly attractive.

Total transaction costs in writing "naked" CBOE calls can be substantial. Brokerage commissions amount to 15% of premiums received, or some 79% of the average gross return from writing such "naked" call options.

COVERED CBOE CALL WRITING

Table IX displays the picture of the actuarial calculations of the average results of typical sales of covered call options on all common stocks listed on the New York Stock Exchange during the 1926-73 period, assuming Chicago Board Option contract terms. In those 29 years when the market advanced, the option holders would have exercised their calls so that the gain on the covering shares would have been limited to the 4.7% dividends retained by the option writers. In the 19 years when the market declined, the premium income was reduced by the loss on the covering shares. After deducting brokerage commissions paid on the options, the average net return from writing covered CBOE call options would have amounted to 14.1% of the initial value of the optioned stock (or 70.5% of the premiums received).

The total return on covered call writing of Chicago Board Options thus would be greater than investment in the portfolio of the underlying stocks alone. The covered call writer receives substantial option premiums in addition to the return on the common stock portfolio.

TABLE IX

Returns to Covered Call Writers on the Chicago Board Options Exchange

(as % of initial share price)

1926—1973

(1) Average loss on exercise of calls in years of market rise 27.0

(2) Average return on covering share in years of market rise 31.7

(3) Average return in years of market rise (2) —(1) 4.7

(4) Average loss on exercise of calls in years of market decline 0

(5) Average loss on covering share in years of market decline 14.4

(6) Weighted average loss .4 x (5) —.6 x (3) 2.9

(7) Average premiums received 20.0

(8) Average returns from writing covered calls (8) —(7) 17.1

(9) Brokerage commissions paid 3.0

(10) Average net return from writing covered calls (9) —(10)........... 14.1

CONCLUSIONS

1. Unless the objective is hedging or insurance, put or call buying generally results in large losses on investment in options.
2. In contrast to the commonly poor results of option buying, certain option writing strategies can attain substantially larger returns on investment than a buy and hold strategy.
3. By the sale of puts, an option writer can in effect regularly acquire shares of stock below their current market prices.
4. Through the sale of covered calls, an option writer can in effect rather regularly sell shares of stock above their current market prices.
5. The sale of "naked" or uncovered call options, however, is not clearly profitable to option writers.
6. By combining the sale of both puts and calls, covered straddle writing can achieve large returns on investment, amounting to some 24% per annum.
7. As an adjunct to regular investment activities, writing of options against a diversified portfolio of securities can produce substantially larger returns on investment than the ordinary buy and hold strategy.

CHAPTER 4

Option Value

While the average rate of return on the purchase or sale of options clearly varies with the type of option contract as well as with the strategy selected, the actual return for a buyer or seller also depends upon the premiums paid for the actuarial value of the options. The spread between the premiums and the actuarial value of the options may make the difference between profit or loss for the buyer or seller. Buyers who generally pay premiums for options in excess of their actuarial values must suffer losses. Conversely, option writing can be profitable only if the premiums received exceed actuarial values of options sold. Whether or not option buyers or sellers gain or lose depends on option premiums. Thus, the option price or premium is an all-important key element in an option transaction.

Options to buy or sell shares of common stock derive their value from the price of the underlying shares. The value of an option is the difference between the expected value of exercising the option and the cost of the option. Hence, the relationship between the current market price of the underlying stock and the exercise price of the option affects the option price. As the market price of the stock increases, a call becomes more valuable and a put becomes less valuable.

PREMIUM

The price of an option can be conceptually decomposed into its intrinsic value and the premium paid for the option privilege. The spread between the market price of the underlying stock and the exercise price of the option represents the intrinsic value of an option. The premium is the excess of the option price over the intrinsic value of an option. In other words, the price of an option equals the sum total of its intrinsic value plus the premium paid for the option privilege.

Here is a formula for the premium percentage on an option:

$$\text{Premium} = \frac{\text{option price} - \text{intrinsic value}}{\text{price of stock} - \text{option price}}$$

In this formula for calculating the premium percentage on an option, the option price is subtracted from the price of the stock in the denominator, because the option price is received by the writer immediately upon sale of the option and thereby reduces the net amount of the initial investment in the option writing position.

Suppose a $3 option price is paid for a call at $10 on a stock selling at $12. In this case, the $2 spread between the $12 market price and the $10 exercise price is the intrinsic value of the option. The $1 excess of the $3 option price over its $2 intrinsic value represents the option premium. In this example, here is how the formula for the premium percentage on this option is calculated:

$$\text{Premium} = \frac{3 - 2}{12 - 3} = 11.1\%$$

62

When a stock is selling below the exercise price of the call option, there is of course no positive intrinsic value. In such event, the call option premium is the sum total of the option price plus the excess of the exercise price over the market price of the stock. For instance, suppose a $1 option price is paid for a call at $10 per share on a stock selling at $8. Since the $2 spread between the $8 market price and the $10 exercise price represents a negative intrinsic value, the $1 option price plus the $2 negative intrinsic value equals a $3 total option premium. In effect, this option holder would be paying a total price of $11 for a stock selling at $8, so that the difference between the total price (the premium plus the exercise price) and the market price of the stock is the total option premium payable by the option holder.

LEVERAGE

A buyer of an option is willing to pay a premium over its intrinsic value, because an option is a way of acquiring leverage. While the price of the option will move with the price of the underlying stock, the percentage changes in the price of the option will be greater than the percentage changes in the price of the underlying stock. For instance, a call at 20 on a stock selling at 25 has an intrinsic value of 5. If the price of the stock rises 100% to 50, the intrinsic value of the call increases 500% to 30.

Similarly, suppose a stock is equally likely to fluctuate from a price of $10 to either $11 or $9 and hence the intrinsic value of a call on this stock at an exercise price of $9 is equally likely to move from $1 to either $2 or zero. Both the stock and the option are subject to a $1 swing in either direction, but $1 on the $1 intrinsic value of the call is ten times the percentage swing of $1 on the $10 price of the optioned stock. In this instance, the option has ten times the percentage volatility or leverage of the underlying stock. Inasmuch as $1 invested in the option could return as much as $10 invested in the stock, the leverage is surely of some value to the option holder.

63

An option not only enhances percentage variability or volatility, but also limits the amount of the potential loss to the cost of the option. Suppose the stock is equally likely to fluctuate from the price of $10 to either $12 or $8 and hence the intrinsic value of a call on this stock at $9 is equally likely to move from $1 to either $3 or to zero. Both the stock and the option are subject to a $2 swing on the upside, but the loss in the intrinsic value of the call is limited to $1 on the downside. In this instance, although the call still has ten times the percentage volatility of the underlying stock on the upside, it has only five times the volatility of the stock on the downside. Since the option leverage works less in one direction than the other, it is not simply a two-edged sword. An option actually provides enhanced variability as well as limited risk.[1]

Since the underlying stock must make a substantial move in the desired direction just to recover the cost of the option before it can yield a profit, the premium paid for the apparent leverage actually reduces the effective leverage. To illustrate, suppose a $2 option price is paid for a call at $9 on a stock selling at $10 and that the price of the stock rises to $11 by the end of the option period. In this instance, despite the 10% increase in the price of the stock, there is no gain in the option value, so that the realized leverage is zero. The effective leverage is measured as the ratio of the percentage change in the option price to the percentage change in the stock price.

Rising premiums result in reduced leverage. After the price of the stock surpasses the exercise price, the premium value of the option tends to diminish as the intrinsic value of the option increases. The loss in premium value thus reflects the reduced leverage of the option.

LIFE OF OPTION

An option generally sells at a premium over its intrinsic value until it is exercised or expires. The premium value tends to decline

---

[1] Paul A. Samuelson, "Rational Theory of Warrant Pricing," *Industrial Management Review*, Spring 1965, p. 21.

as the remaining life of the option diminishes. At its expiration date, an option sells at no more than its intrinsic value. If an option has no intrinsic value, it expires worthless.

Option life or time remaining before expiration is obviously an important factor affecting option premium. An option is worth more when a long period of time remains before expiration than when only a short period of time remains until its expiration date. For instance, a distant October call option for a particular stock normally commands a larger premium than an otherwise identical April option, since the holder of the October call has an additional six months for the underlying stock to advance in price. As the expiration date of the near option approaches, its option value will decline toward zero unless the price of the underlying stock exceeds the exercise price of the option.

As a matter of fact, the value of an option or any short-lived warrant increases proportionally with the square-root of time remaining before expiration.[2] For example, a twelve-month option is worth twice as much as a three-month option, because the price of a stock tends to fluctuate twice as widely over a twelve-month period than over a three-month period. Similarly, since the square root of 4 equals 2, a four-month option is expected to sell at twice the price of an otherwise identical one-month option. Expected price changes are smaller as the duration of the contract diminishes.

VOLATILITY

Since the option buyer acquires leverage and his potential loss is limited to the cost of the option no matter how much the price of the underlying stock fluctuates, the value of an option tends to increase with an increase in the expected variance or volatility in the price of the underlying stock. If the price of a particular com-

---

[2] Louis Bachelier, "Theory of Speculation, 1900," in *The Random Character of Stock Market Prices,* Paul H. Cootner, ed. (Cambridge, Mass.: M.I.T. Press, 1964), pp. 17-78.

mon stock normally swing widely, an option on that stock is likely to command a larger premium than an option on a stock than usually trades in a narrow price range. Through this functional relationship, the faster the stock price rises, the faster the call option price rises.[3]

Indeed, there is a positive relationship between premium paid for options and the variability of stock prices. The volatility of prices of underlying stocks is a most significant factor accounting for option premiums.[4] Even a risk averter "would be willing to pay a positive price for leverage in order to gain a higher expected return" and an increase in the expected risk of a stock will result in a higher expected value of the option.[5]

RISK

Total risk can be decomposed into the risk due to the stock's inherent volatility and the risk due to its sensitivity to fluctuations in the general market. In a widely diversified portfolio, fluctuations arising out of inherent volatility (dependent on specific developments within the company) tend to offset or cancel one another, since some stocks rise while others decline. But the systematic risk associated with fluctuations in the general market cannot be eliminated through diversification since it is common to all securities.[6]

A measure of a stock's relative sensitivity to fluctuations in the general market averages is the Beta coefficient. The Beta factor is an average rate of change relative to the general market movement, showing how fast an individual stock (or portfolio) moves up or down relative to the general market movement. A Beta coefficient of 2 indicates that the stock will tend to move twice as fast as the

[3] Fischer Black and Myron Scholes, "The Pricing of Options and Corporate Liabilities," *Journal of Political Economy*, May-June 1973, p. 644.

[4] Burton G. Malkiel and Richard E. Quandt, *Strategies and Rational Decisions in the Securities Option Market* (Cambridge, Mass.: M.I.T. Press, 1969), pp. 27-31.

[5] Case M. Sprenkle, "Warrant Prices as Indicators of Expectations and Preferences," *Yale Economic Essays*, 1961, pp. 178-231.

[6] Frank B. Campanella, *The Measurement of Portfolio Risk Exposure: Use of Beta Coefficient* (Lexington, Mass.: D. C. Heath, 1972), pp. 11-14.

general market. If the general market average rises 10%, this stock could be expected to rise 20% in response to the market movement alone. Conversely, if the market declines 10%, this stock could be expected to decline 20%. A Beta of 1 indicates that the stock is as volatile as the market average.

In addition to the general market risk of a stock as measured by its Beta coefficient, a stock has its own residual risk due to its inherent volatility that is independent of the general market. This measure of a stock's own inherent volatility, which can be eliminated through diversification, is called the Alpha coefficient. The addition of the Alpha coefficient plus the Beta coefficient equals a stock's total risk or volatility.

The option premium depends on the total variance in the common stock. The greater the volatility or the more risky the security, the more valuable is the option.[7]

While the volatility of underlying stock prices is a most significant variable accounting for option premiums, the effect of differences in the variance rate on the actuarial value of an option tends to be undervalued in the market. "Market traders systematically underestimate the value of an option on a high variance security and systematically overestimate the value of an option on a low variance security."[8]

In other words, premiums paid for options on very volatile stocks generally do not provide writers with adequate compensation for the additional risk involved in such stocks. The risk premiums are not strictly proportional to their Beta coefficients. Returns on stocks with high Betas are smaller than expected on the basis of risk. Stocks with lower Beta coefficients tend to be more rewarding than those with higher factors.[9]

[7] Robert C. Merton, "The Theory of Rational Option Pricing," *Bell Journal of Economics and Management Science,* Spring 1973, pp. 148-149.

[8] Fischer Black and Myron Scholes, "The Valuation of Option Contracts and a Test of Market Efficiency," *Journal of Finance,* May 1972, pp. 399-417.

[9] Fischer Black, Michael C. Jensen and Myron S. Scholes, "The Capital Asset Pricing Model: Some Empirical Tests" in *Studies in the Theory of Capital Markets,* Michael C. Jensen, ed. (New York: Praeger, 1972.)

PRICE OF STOCK

Premium percentages tend to be inversely related to market prices of the underlying shares of stock, so that low priced shares generally command larger premium percentages than high priced shares. The ratio of the option premium to the market price of a stock varies inversely with the price of the stock for two reasons: An option buyer typically prefers to limit his risk to only a small amount of funds and hence favors lower priced shares. At the same time, an option writer usually insists on a larger premium percentage on lower priced shares, because the transaction costs including brokerage commissions are generally a larger percentage of the market price of the underlying stock on lower priced shares than on higher priced shares. Therefore, low priced stocks command larger premium percentages.[10]

PUTS VERSUS CALLS

The standard over-the-counter option contract stipulates that "during the life of this option, the contract price shall be reduced by the value of any cash dividend on the day the stock goes ex-dividend." This dividend treatment favors the holder of a call as well as the writer of a put. Conversely, this dividend provision in over-the-counter option contracts works against the holder of a put and the writer of a call.[11]

This treatment of dividends significantly enhances the value of calls, but diminishes the value of puts in conventional over-the-counter option contracts. In fact, the actuarial value of calls are increased about 24% and the actuarial value of puts are decreased 27% "from what they otherwise would have been."[12]

However, the exercise price of a listed option is not adjusted for

---

[10] U.S. Securities and Exchange Commission, *Report on Put and Call Options,* 1961, p. 41.

[11] Richard J. Kruizenga, "Profit Returns from Purchasing Puts and Calls" in *The Random Character of Stock Market Prices,* Paul H. Cootner, ed. (Cambridge, Mass.: M.I.T. Press, 1964), pp. 402-403.

[12] *Ibid.,* p. 410.

any ordinary cash dividends on the underlying stock, since the option writer is entitled to retain such dividends during the life of the call option. This dividend provision makes listed call options generally less valuable than conventional call options traded in the over-the-counter option market. Consequently, the average premium of 12% of the value of the stock received by writers of six-month over-the-counter calls is in effect the equivalent of some 10% on CBOE calls.

Since the holder of a listed option does not receive the right to dividend payments during the life of the option and since the price of the underlying stock is likely to decline by the amount of the dividend on an ex-dividend day, a listed call option on a high dividend yielding security cannot be as valuable generally as a call on a low dividend yielding security.

It is expected that when puts will be traded on the Chicago Board Options Exchange, there will be no provision for any adjustment to the exercise price for any ordinary cash dividends on the underlying stock during the life of the option. Since the put option holder will be entitled to retain any dividends received during the life of the option contract, a CBOE put will be more valuable than a put traded in the over-the-counter market.

Since stock prices cannot fall below zero but are unbounded from above, this asymmetry would generally make calls somewhat more valuable than puts. Nevertheless, the possibility of option arbitrage will tend to establish a ceiling on the spread between put and call premiums.[13]

---

[13] Hans R. Stoll, "The Relationship Between Put and Call Option Prices," *Journal of Finance*, Dec. 1969, pp. 801-824.

DETERMINANTS OF OPTION VALUE

The most important determinants or ingredients of option values for various types of option contracts are:

1. the relationship of the price of the underlying stock to the exercise price of the option,
2. the remaining life of the option

    and

3. the volatility of the underlying stock.

While the amount of the spread between the premiums and actuarial values may make the difference between profit or loss for the buyer or seller of any type of option contract, the actual return on investment clearly varies with the strategy selected.

CHAPTER 5

Selective Strategy

Investors can substantially improve their portfolio performance by engaging in a variety of option strategies. While some strategies by their very nature are clearly speculative, option writing is especially attractive for conservative investors. Institutional investors in particular may improve investment performance considerably by writing or selling options against common stocks in their portfolios, instead of simply holding a diversified portfolio.

Options are employed for various purposes. Basically, an option is bought to maximize the possible profit in an investment or speculation, while minimizing the risk or limiting the loss to the cost of the option. A put purchase may be employed as a hedge against an investment position in the underlying stock or as a speculation on a fall in the price of the stock. A call may be bought as a hedge against a short position in the related stock, or as a speculation on a rise in the price of the stock.

71

Writers generally sell various options in order to receive premiums and achieve a larger return on capital. Puts are sold by writers willing to acquire stocks below their current market prices. Covered calls are sold by writers willing to sell stocks above their current market prices. Writers, who are willing either to acquire stocks below their current market prices or to sell stocks above their current market prices, sell straddles. Thus, it is in the nature of option selling that the writer tends to dispose of stocks after a rise and to accumulate shares when they are depressed—a sound investment strategy.

The sale of an uncovered or "naked" call might be used as a speculation on a fall in the price of the related stock, but is vulnerable to the risk of unlimited loss. The sale of a so-called covered put presents a speculative risk similar to uncovered or "naked" call writing, because the short position in the underlying stock is also vulnerable to the possibility of unlimited losses. On the other hand, the risk involved in writing an uncovered or "naked" put resembles that of covered call writing. The writer of either a put or a covered call incurs the risk of loss from a fall in the price of the underlying stock, except that this risk is reduced by the amount of the premium received.

CALL BUYING

An option is a way of acquiring leverage. A given amount of funds may purchase a call covering a much larger quantity of stock than could be bought directly, because the price of an option is considerably less than the cost of the underlying stock. Since the price of an option moves with the price of the underlying stock, the percentage changes in the price of the option are always greater than the percentage change in the price of the stock. This leverage potential enables a call buyer to benefit from a rise in the price of the stock to a substantially greater extent than from the outright purchase of the stock. However, the entire investment in the option is lost if the price of the stock does not rise, whereas direct

72

purchase of the stock might incur no loss or only a paper loss. The holder of a call cannot wait for an upturn in the stock price beyond the option's expiration date. Moreover, for a call to be profitable, the optioned stock must appreciate in value by an amount exceeding the premium plus commissions.

Nonetheless, the potential profit opportunity for the holder of a call is unlimited, whereas the possible loss on the transaction is limited to the price paid for the option. Since the buyer cannot lose more than the cost of the option no matter how much the price of the underlying stock drops, the value of a call increases with the expected variance or instability in the price of the under-lying security. The more volatile the price of a stock, the more valuable is an option on that stock.

Therefore, the very stock considered conservative as an outright purchase might be more risky as an option speculation. For example, a stable security is commonly considered a safer investment than a volatile stock since its market value is less likely to fall, but the same stability also indicates that its price is less likely to rise substantially during the relatively short life of the option.

Option buyers favor calls on stocks likely to have wide price swings in relation to premium costs, since such calls can attain considerable upside profit potential with the risk limited to the cost of the options. While they seek volatile vehicles in order to maximize leverage, the payment of larger premiums could mean a lower return for the option holder. To illustrate, suppose the price of the underlying stock rises 20% and the premium paid for the call was 10% of the exercise price, so that the return (before commissions) amounted to 100%. In such a transaction, if the premium paid were 20% instead of 10%, there would have been no net return at all. Clearly, the option price is an all-important determinant of the rate of return on the purchase of options.

Unless the price of the underlying stock rises by an amount ex-ceeding the cost of the call, the option holder must suffer a loss on the option. The rate of return on options could indeed be improved by acquiring calls on very volatile vehicles at premiums below their actuarial values. In fact, not only does the value of an option increase with an increase in the expected variance or volatility in the underlying stock, but the premium paid for an option on a high variance or volatile stock is generally smaller than its actuarial value.[1]

The purchase of a call can serve as a substitute for buying securities on margin. Holding a call costing 10% of the price of the underlying stock is like buying the stock on 10% margin. By putting up only 10%, the option holder acquires the potential profit on ten times as many shares as could be obtained by outright purchase of the stock. In effect, the leverage is achieved on extremely small margin.

A call option may be bought either as a hedge against a short position in the related stock, or as a speculation on a rise in the price of the stock. As a speculation, a call can maximize the possible profit, while minimizing the risk or limiting the loss to the cost of the option.

CALL WRITING

Indirectly, a call buyer acquires leverage from the option writer, who assumes the obligation to deliver the shares of the underlying stock against payment of the exercise price should the shares be called. The call option writer may employ either one of two alternative strategies:

1. The "naked" or uncovered call writer sells the call option without any position in the underlying stock,

or

2. The covered call writer owns or purchases the stock against which the call option is written.

---

[1] Fischer Black and Myron Scholes, "The Valuation of Option Contracts and a Test of Market Efficiency," *Journal of Finance*, May 1972, p. 408.

The covered call writer foregoes the opportunity for gain from a rise in the price of the stock above the exercise price in return for the premium received, but retains the risk of a loss from a fall in the price of the stock. This downside risk is not newly acquired, if he sells calls on stock already in his portfolio. In fact, this downside risk is reduced by the amount of the premium.

In contrast, the risk to a "naked" or uncovered call writer is that the price of the stock might rise above the combined amount of the exercise price plus the premium. This upside risk to the "naked" call writer is somewhat similar to the downside risk of a covered call writer.

The "naked" call writer is required to deposit margin to cover some portion of the value of the underlying stock. If the price of the stock does not rise sufficiently to cover the transaction costs of the option buyer or the price of the stock declines, the option is not exercised and the writer simply pockets the full amount of the premium received.

The return on a "naked" or uncovered call is calculated on the basis of the amount of the initial margin required. An annual yield formula for a "naked" call option is:

$$\text{Yield} = \frac{\text{premium X frequency}}{\text{margin required} - \text{premium}}$$

The frequency is the number of possible times per year the premium might be received by the writer. Thus, the frequency on a two-month option would be 6; a three-month 4; a six-month 2; and a year 1.

For example, on the sale of a six-month "naked" call on 100 shares of U.S. Steel at $40 for a $400 premium requiring 50% margin, this yield formula is calculated as follows:

$$\text{Yield} = \frac{400 \text{ X } 2}{2,000 - 400} = 50\%$$

This yield, of course, would represent the gross return, assuming the call will not be exercised. If the price of the stock rises sufficiently to make the call worth exercising, the "naked" option writer must buy the stock to fulfill his contractual obligation. In addition to the purchase price of the shares, the writer pays the costs of two transactions: first, the brokerage commission for buying the stock and second, the transaction costs in selling the stock to the option holder.

Like short selling, "naked" call writing is very vulnerable to a substantial rise in the price of the underlying stock. The potential loss of an uncovered call writer theoretically has no limit. Since uncovered call writing is so clearly and completely exposed to unlimited risk, some say that "naked" call writing is like students streaking.

The covered call writer, on the other hand, runs relatively limited risk. Should the price of the underlying stock rise and the option is exercised, the writer simply sells his stock at the exercise price to fulfill the option contract. The option writer receives the proceeds of the sale amounting to the exercise price plus the call premium minus commissions.

The return on a covered call is calculated on the basis of the amount invested in the underlying stock. An annual yield formula for a covered call option is:

$$\text{Yield} = \frac{\text{premium X frequency}}{\text{cost of 100 shares — premium}}$$

For example, on the sale of a six-month covered call on 100 shares of U.S. Steel at $40 for a $400 premium, this yield formula is calculated as follows:

$$\text{Yield} = \frac{400 \text{ X } 2}{4,000 - 400} = 22.2\%$$

This yield, of course, would represent the gross return on the covered call. Transaction costs including brokerage commissions could reduce the gross yield.

76

If the price of the shares declines, the covered call writer at least has earned the option premium to offset to that extent the loss in market value of the stock. In this way, the covered call writer is surely in a better investment position than the investor who employs a strategy of buying and holding the same shares, without engaging in option writing.

Either way the market moves, the covered call option writer is ahead. Should the price of the stock decline, the receipt of the premium helps compensate for a loss in market value. If the price of the stock rises, the total of the proceeds from the sale of the shares plus the option premium received must exceed the proceeds from the sale of the shares alone. Writing covered call options generally provides larger investment returns and less risk than holding a diversified portfolio alone. The bulk of call writing is done on a covered basis with additional return and hedging as the primary objectives.

When writing covered call options, the following minimum annual yield bases might be employed:

TABLE X

Expected Gross Yield on Covered Call Writing

Duration	Premium Percentage	Frequency	Gross Yield
One year	16	1	16%
6 months	10	2	20%
3 months	7	4	28%
2 months	6	6	36%
1 month	5	12	60%

An option writer has no business dealing in securities which he does not want to own. On the other hand, where the investor does not want to sell a particular security under any circumstances, a call option must not be sold at all. To prevent undue risks caused by fluctuations in the market prices of individual stocks, the option writer should diversify his securities portfolio. To limit undue risks associated with general market movements, the option writer must stagger option sales over a period of time. Option expirations should not be concentrated in any single month or two.

In order to reduce risks of extreme fluctuations in the prices of individual stocks, high variance or very volatile stocks must be avoided and low variance or stable securities must be favored. A writer's profit on an option transaction is largest when the price of the underlying stock does not move at all or changes so little that the option expires unexercised, so that holding the covering stock does not absorb any loss. While the profit to the call option writer is limited to the amount of the premium received, there is a possible loss if the price of the underlying stock drops more than the amount of the premium. Since the covered call writer cannot possibly lose unless the price of the stock falls by an amount greater than the option premium, options on stocks likely to have narrow price swings should be favored by writers.

By avoiding very volatile stocks, call writing not only reduces risk, but also can achieve a higher rate of return on investment. This is true, because the premium value of an option on a low variance stock is generally overestimated so that premiums paid for options on stable securities "tend to be too high."[2]

Nonetheless, writers expect to be paid larger premiums for options on less stable securities, to compensate for the additional risk. The expected premium on volatile stocks should be more than proportionate to the Beta factor. For instance, if the expected premium on an average six-month call is 10% and the Beta coefficient on the particular stock under option is twice the average, then the expected premium on such a volatile stock should be at least 20% of the price of the stock.

---

[2] *Ibid.*

In summary, covered call writing is an attractive strategy serving as a means of selling shares above their current market prices. Writing of calls against a portfolio of securities can boost investment return substantially.

PUT PURCHASE

A put purchase may be employed as a hedge against an investment in the underlying stock or as a speculation on a fall in the price of the stock. As a hedge, should the price of the stock drop, the put could limit the loss on the investment to the cost of the option. As a speculation, the put can benefit from leverage if the price of the stock falls. On the other hand, if the price of the stock rises, the loss is limited to the cost of the option.

A put purchase can be a useful substitute for a short sale. Compared to the alternative of selling short, put purchases are particularly attractive because of their predetermined or limited risk as well as their leveraged potential for a much greater return. A short sale incurs an extremely high risk, because the possible loss is unlimited should the price of the stock rise. The potential profit, nevertheless, is limited to a maximum of 100%. Moreover, any profit on a short sale is considered a short-term gain for tax purposes, no matter how long the short position remained open. Since a put contract, on the other hand, is considered a capital asset for tax purposes, a put option is the only way possible to convert a profit from a short position into a long-term capital gain.

For instance, on a put purchased on a $50 stock for a $500 premium, the potential loss would be limited to the amount of the premium, but the leverage provides the possibilty of a long-term capital gain up to 900% should the underlying stock become worthless during the option period. In contrast, a short sale of the stock risks unlimited potential loss, but the posible profit is limited to a short-term capital gain of 100% even if the stock becomes worthless.

79

Thus, a put purchase provides the option holder the leverage to benefit from a drop in the price of the stock to a much greater extent than the outright short sale of the stock, without incurring the risk of unlimited loss should the price of the stock rise. However, if the price of the stock does not drop, the put purchaser would lose his entire investment in the option. The put is profitable only if the underlying stock falls in price by an amount exceeding the premium plus commissions.

Since the potential loss on a put purchase is limited to the option price no matter how much the stock price rises, the value of a put increases with the expected variance in the price of the underlying stock. Therefore, the very stock considered speculative as an outright purchase may be much more attractive as a put option, because the price of a stable security is less likely to drop very much during the relatively short duration of the option period. The more volatile the price of a stock, the more valuable is a put option on such stock.

Inasmuch as puts obtain the advantage of the downside potential without incurring an unlimited upside risk, speculative put purchasers favor options on stocks likely to have wide price swings in relation to option prices, in order to maximize leverage. Larger premiums, however, could mean reduced returns to the put holder. For example, suppose a 10% premium were paid for a put on a stock which declined 20% pricewise, so that the return (before commissions) amounted to 100%. However, if the premium paid were 20% instead of 10%, there would be no net return whatsoever. Obviously, the option price is an all-important determinant of the rate of return on put purchases.

Nonetheless, since the value of an option increases with an increase in the expected variance of the price of the underlying stock and the price of an option on a high variance stock is generally too low relative to its actuarial value, put purchasers tend to favor very volatile vehicles for speculative purposes.

PUT WRITING

A put purchaser indirectly acquires leverage from the option writer, who assumes an obligation to buy the underlying stock if the shares are put. If the price of the stock rises, the put writer simply pockets the premium received. If the price drops by an amount greater than the option price, the writer suffers a loss on the transaction. The potential loss on writing a put option, however, is limited by the price of the stock minus the option price.

Uncovered or "naked" put writing is a common strategy for two reasons: Not only is the potential loss on a "naked" put limited by the price of the stock (less the premium received), but a so-called covered put cannot really protect the writer at all. Unlike the long position in the case of a covered call, the combination of writing a put and selling short would make the writer vulnerable to unlimited losses. If the price of the underlying stock rises, the put holder will not exercise his option and the option writer must then cover his short position on unfavorable terms. Typically, therefore, a put writer does not attempt to cover himself by a short sale.

Since puts are commonly written against margin rather than covering stock, an annual yield formula for "naked" put writing is:

$$\text{Yield} = \frac{\text{premium} \times \text{frequency}}{\text{margin required} - \text{premium}}$$

For example, on the sale of a six-month put on 100 shares of U.S. Steel at $40 for a $400 premium requiring 50% margin, this yield formula is calculated as follows:

$$\text{Yield} = \frac{400 \times 2}{2,000 - 400} = 50\%$$

This figure, of course, would represent an optimum or maximum result, before deducting transaction costs. When writing puts, the following annual yield bases might be employed:

81

TABLE XI

Expected Gross Yield on Put Writing

Duration	Premium Percentage	100% Margin Gross Yield	50% Margin Gross Yield
One year	12	12%	24%
6 months	8	16%	32%
3 months	6	24%	48%
2 months	5	30%	60%
1 month	4	48%	96%

Regardless of the promising or prospective yield, an option writer has absolutely no business selling puts on stocks that he does not want to own. Since a put writer is obligated to acquire shares that are put, he is vulnerable to the risk of a loss should the price of the underlying stock drop. Hence, an option must not be sold, if the writer does not want to hold the stock.

A put should be sold only on a stock which the writer would be willing to buy at around the current market price less its option premium. In order to avoid undue risks associated with extreme fluctuation in the prices of underlying stocks, very volatile stocks must be carefully avoided and options on low variance or stable securities should be favored. In fact, should the price of the stock not fluctuate or change at all, the option writer cannot lose. A loss can be realized only if the price of the optioned stock drops more than the amount of the premium received.

Accordingly, writing of puts on stocks with narrow price swings should be favored. By avoiding very volatile vehicles, a put option writer not only reduces risk but can also achieve a larger rate of return on investment, because the price of an option on a low variance stock is generally greater than its actuarial value.[3]

---

[3] Ibid.

As compared with the average put premium percentage, the expected premium on volatile stocks should be more than proportionate to the Beta coefficient, in order to compensate for the greater risk factor. For example, if the expected premium on a typical six-month put is 8% and the Beta coefficient on the particular stock is twice the average, the expected premium on such a volatile stock should amount to at least 16% of the price of the stock.

In any event, an enticing strategy is to write "naked" puts on stocks found attractive for investment, for the purpose of acquiring shares at a lower cost than their current market prices.

STRADDLE WRITING

As a combination of a put and a call option on the same shares, straddle strategy for the option writer involves getting greater premiums than on the sale of individual puts or calls alone. Whereas the dual premium received on a straddle is substantially larger than the premium on a simple call or put, the straddle writer needs neither more margin nor securities than the call writer. A writer, who owns the underlying stock, can sell a straddle as easily as a call, by simply depositing his shares as the required margin for both the put and the call options comprising the straddle. Moreover, straddle writing gets more favorable tax treatment, too, since the premium from a lapsed part of a straddle constitutes a short-term capital gain rather than ordinary income.

The annual yield formula for a covered straddle is the same as for a covered call:

$$\text{Yield} = \frac{\text{premium X frequency}}{\text{cost of 100 shares —premium}}$$

When writing covered straddles, the following minimum annual yield bases might be employed:

Table XII

Expected Gross Yield on Covered Straddle Writing

Duration	Percentage Premium	Frequency	Gross Yield
One year	25	1	25%
6 months	16	2	32%
3 months	12	4	48%
2 months	10	6	60%
1 month	8	12	96%

Of course, the writer of straddles should expect to receive even higher percentage premiums on the sale of options on volatile stocks, as extra compensation for the greater risk factor. But no option at all should be sold if the writer is not interested in either buying or selling a particular stock under any circumstances.

An investor who regularly writes covered straddles against stocks in his portfolio can considerably improve his investment return. As the prices of some stocks rise, the call sides of the straddles are exercised by the option holders, so that the sales proceeds include the striking prices plus the premiums received. On the other hand, as prices of some stocks decline, the put sides of the straddles are exercised by the option holders, so that the premium receipts reduce the acquisition costs of the securities purchased. In this manner, additional shares are acquired at lower costs and conversely shares are sold at higher prices.

Based on past results, the best strategy involves the sale of straddles against a diversified portfolio of quality common stocks. This is a much better strategy than simply holding a diversified portfolio.

84

CONVERTIBLE SECURITIES

With the exception of "naked" call writing, option selling assumes the risk of loss stemming from a precipitous fall in the market price of the underlying securities during the life of the option. If the price of the stock declines, for example, a call will expire unexercised, but the value of the shares will be worth less than the market price at the time the option was written. Although the option premium acts as a buffer against loss to the extent of the amount of the premium received by the writer and thus absorbs normal or most market fluctuations, an extraordinary drop in the market price could still result in a net loss on the underlying security.

In order to provide a better buffer or much greater protection against the risk of loss on the underlying security held in the portfolio, ownership of a convertible bond can be used to support either a call or straddle option on the stock. The use of the convertible bond for covered option writing has an advantage in that there is generally less risk in owning convertible bonds than in holding the related stock. If the price of the underlying stock drops, the decline in the price of the convertible bond is limited by its investment value as a bond.[4]

Therefore, for almost complete protection against a fall in the price of the stock, the price of the bond must be supported by its investment value as a "straight" bond. For almost complete protection against a rise in the price of the stock, the ideal convertible must be purchased with the conversion parity value equal to its striking price. The price of the convertible bond will not necessarily advance along with its stock price, if its conversion parity exceeds the stock's market price. If the price of the convertible bond exceeds its "straight" investment value, it will also decline along with its underlying stock, especially if the bond market

---

[4] Charles L. Hubbard and Terry Johnson, "Profits from Writing Calls with Convertible Bonds," *Financial Analysts Journal*, Nov.-Dec. 1969, pp. 78-89.

tumbles as interest rates rise. A convertible bond is used to cover a call when it has greater resistance to a downturn than the related stock.

Although convertible bonds seldom serve as perfect protection for covered call writing, there is generally less risk in owning convertible bonds than in holding the related stock. If the stock is called, the bonds could be converted and the shares delivered. Similarly, convertible preferred stock and also possibly warrants may be used. In fact, options are sometimes written on warrants instead of common stock.

Both convertible bonds and preferred stock can provide better downside protection than the underlying stock. Convertible bonds, moreover, are acceptable in lieu of the underlying stock in a covered call option under the rules of the New York Stock Exchange. But neither convertible preferred stock nor warrants may be substituted for the underlying stock as a covered call. When warrants are available, options may be written on a warrant itself. Such an option, in effect, is an option on an option, since a warrant is really a long-term call option.

Whether one uses common stock or convertible bonds or preferred stock or even warrants, the writing of options against a portfolio is no more speculative than owning such securities. A covered call option writer, for instance, runs relatively minimal risk. The option writer sells stock at prices higher than the current market. On the other hand, when stock prices decline, the covered call writer is left with less valuable shares, but has been compensated at least by option premium income. Those who simply own the same securities do not have any buffer to offset their losses. Hence, covered option writing may be less risky and more profitable than investment in a diversified portfolio of common stock.

Obviously, an option writer has no business dealing in securities that he would not want to own and must have the necessary resources to honor all options written. The necessary resources may comprise cash or its equivalent including Governments as well as tax-exempt municipals and other bonds in addition to stock.

CHAPTER 6

Tax Tactics

What you get is not exactly what you keep. Since income tax laws and regulations determine how much of any income can be retained, any attempt to maximize the net return on investment must focus on the tax status of any security transaction. The net return on investment can be enhanced by either legally avoiding a tax liability, or reducing the tax, or deferring the tax liability to a future year.[1]

TAX EXEMPT

Income tax liability may be avoided by investing in tax-exempt securities. Interest income on all securities issued by states or their subdivisions is exempt from federal income taxes, as well as from any state or local income taxes if such securities were issued in

---

[1] Jack Crestol, Herman M. Schneider and Warren G. Wintrub, *Investor's Tax Savings Guide* (Princeton, N. J.: Dow Jones Books, 1970).

the state that the investor claims domicile or permanent legal residence. The exemption from federal income taxes, however, is not applicable to capital gains on these securities. Neither does this tax exemption apply to federal estate and gift taxes.[2]

For example, if an investor in the 50% income tax bracket purchases a municipal bond yielding 5%, the return on this tax-free bond comes to a taxable equivalent yield of 10%. This federal income tax exemption is the valuable feature drawing special attraction to state and municipal securities, because high income tax rates cut considerably the net return (after taxes) on all other bonds. This tax exemption, however, also tends to reduce available interest rates on municipal securities as against yields on other bonds of comparable quality or risk.

The specific exemption of interest income on state and municipal securities is provided in the Internal Revenue Code, but the Sixteenth Amendment to the United States Constitution clearly gives Congress the power to "levy and collect taxes on incomes, from whatever sources derived." Hence, there may be some uncertainty whether interest income on municipals will remain tax-free forever.

CAPITAL GAINS

Tax liability may be reduced by such legitimate means as converting short-term profits into long-term capital gains, which are generally profits realized from the sale of securities or other capital assets owned longer than six months. Long-term capital gains are taxable at half the rate applicable to ordinary income, while short-term gains are taxed at the same rate as ordinary income.

In the initial computation, long-term gains are matched against long-term losses to produce a net long-term gain or loss. Similarly, short-term gains are matched against short-term losses to produce

[2] Albert I. A. Bookbinder, *Investment Decision-Making* (Elmont, N. Y.: Programmed Press, 1968), pp. 90-94.

a net short-term gain or loss. Then net long-term gains are reduced by net short-term losses, or net short-term gains are reduced by net long-term losses.

In computing the tax, only one-half of the excess of net long-term gains over net short-term losses is taxed like ordinary income, but net short-term gains in excess of net long-term losses are fully taxed like ordinary income. If there is a net capital loss, the amount deductible against ordinary income is limited to $1,000 for the year. In the case of an excess of long-term capital losses over capital gains, only half of the loss may be deducted from ordinary income. Therefore, $2,000 in net long-term capital losses is needed to offset $1,000 of other income. Capital losses in excess of these limits may be carried forward to future years, but the losses retain their short-term or long-term character.

Since net short-term gains in excess of net long-term capital losses are fully taxable like ordinary income and only one-half of the excess of net long-term capital gains over short-term losses is in effect treated like ordinary income, securities which have appreciated in value should be held longer than six months. Likewise, realizing both long-term gains and losses in the same year should generally be avoided. Transactions should be arranged so that short-term gains are deductible against long-term losses.

Here is an illustration of favorable tax treatment of long-term capital gains: Suppose an investor in the 50% income tax bracket realizes a $100,000 long-term capital gain and a $50,000 short-term loss, so that the net long-term capital gain (before taxes) is $50,000. Since only half of this net amount is taxable at the regular rate, he pays a tax of $12,500. This amounts to an effective tax rate of only 25%. In other words, a net long-term capital gain is virtually worth twice as much as ordinary income.

Hence, an investor's tax strategy is to make any losses short-term and any profits long-term capital gains.

DEFERRING TAX

If an investment shows substantial capital appreciation but the investor's tax position will be much more favorable the suceeding year, the tax liability on the capital gain can be deferred by "selling short against the box." This is done by selling short an equal number of shares and covering the short sale the following year by delivering the shares originally held. In this way, the capital gain is carried over into the succeeding year. The short-term or long-term nature of the gain is not at all affected by the deferral of the tax liability, since its nature is determined at the time of the short sale.

For instance, if an investor wished to protect his profit on stock acquired on May 3, 1974 for $10 per share and priced at $20 on December 16, 1974, this stock could have been sold short at $20 to defer the closing of this sales transaction until January 1975. At that time, the long-term capital gain of $10 per share (less transactions costs) would have been realized for income tax purposes, by delivering the shares originally held to close the short position. If this stock had not been held longer than six-months at the time of the short sale, the profit would have been considered short-term rather than a long-term capital gain.

A basic tax rule is that a long-term capital gain cannot be realized from a short sale. No matter how long a short position is maintained, selling short cannot receive long-term tax treatment, since such sale precedes purchase. Statutory rules effectively prevent the use of short sales to convert short-term profits into long-term capital gains when the investor holds other securities substantially identical to the securities sold short. No long-term capital gain may be realized if such stock is held short-term at the time of the short sale or acquired after the short sale is made and before it is closed.

Any loss on the sale of a security is deferred under the wash sale rule if such security is reacquired or a call option on such security is purchased within a 30 day period before or after such sale.[3]

OPTIONS

A put or call option is considered a capital asset for federal income tax purposes. The cost of an option purchase is a capital expenditure, so that the tax treatment of an option depends on its disposition. Upon the sale of the option, the difference between the proceeds and the cost of the option is treated as a capital gain or loss. If the option has not been held longer than six months, the gain or loss is deemed "short-term." If the holding period was longer than six-months, the gain or loss is treated as "long-term." If an option is allowed to lapse without being exercised, its expiration is treated as a sale and its cost constitutes a capital loss on the expiration date. This loss is deemed short-term or long-term capital loss, depending upon the holding period of the option.

CALLS

The tax consequences of the purchase of a call option are delayed until the transaction is closed. If the buyer of a call allows it to lapse without being exercised, its expiration is treated as a sale and the cost of the option constitutes a capital loss on the date of expiration. If the call option is sold, the difference between the proceeds and the cost of the option is treated as a capital gain or loss. If the call is exercised, the cost of this option is added to the cost of the acquired stock. The exercise of the call starts the holding period for the acquired stock, so that the holding period of the stock does not include the holding period of the exercised call. No capital gain or loss is realized until the acquired stock is sold.

The treatment of a call option as a capital asset permits its holder to obtain tax advantages. For instance, if an appreciated

---

[3] Section 1091 of the Internal Revenue Code.

190-day call option has been held less than six months, the holder can protect the profit against a market decline by selling short the underlying stock, thus freezing the profit. If the call is still profit- able after the six-month holding period, the option may be sold to establish the long-term capital gain and the short sale closed out for a short-term gain or loss. If the price of the underlying stock continues its rise, the sale of the option results in an even larger long-term capital gain and the closing of the short position pro- duces a short-term loss. This transaction is not tainted by any short sale restriction rules, because the call and the underlying stock are not considered substantially identical securities.

On the other hand, assume that after a 190-day call on 100 shares of U.S. Steel at $40 per share is purchased, the market price of these shares falls, so that this option becomes worthless at the end of six months. The sale of the "worthless" call to an option dealer for a nominal price of $1 just before the end of six months would create a short-term capital loss, which could be deducted from short-term capital gains taxable at ordinary rates If this investor is in the 50% income tax bracket, the establish- ment of this short-term loss would thus provide an out-of-pocket loss of 50%. In contrast, if the loss had been allowed to become long-term, it would have offset long-term capital gains taxable at a more favorable 25% rate. Thus, by establishing a short-term loss deductible against short-term gains, a tax benefit of 25% would be obtained.

However, if the price of the optioned stock rises from $40 to $60 per share by the end of six months, the option holder must not exercise this profitable call. This would merely start the holding period for the acquired stock, so that a long-term capital gain might not be realized. Instead of exercising the call, this option could be sold after the six-month holding period to a third party for its market value, in order to realize a long-term capital gain.

By utilizing optimal tax tactics, an option buyer is able to treat losses as short-term capital losses and to establish profits as long-term capital gains. For instance, an investor in the 70% income tax bracket could qualify his losses on unprofitable options as off-sets against short-term gains taxable at the 70% rate and his gains on profitable options as long-term capital gainst taxable at the more favorable 35% rate. Suppose the probability that an option will appreciate 80% is .5 and that the probability that it will expire unexercised is .5. Then the expected value of this option is

$$.5 \ (.8) + .5 \ (-1) = -10\%$$

Assuming the existence of other short-term gains taxable at 70% and long-term gains taxable at 35%, the after-tax expected value would be

$$.5 \ (.8) \ (1-.35) + .5 \ (-1) \ (1-.7) = +11\%$$

Whereas the pre-tax expected value is a negative 10% in this case, the peculiarities of the income tax law favorable to long-term capital gains produce an after-tax expectation of a positive 11%.

The sharp contrast between the pre-tax expected value and the post-tax expected value of an option tends to be even greater to the extent that the prices of the optioned stocks are more volatile rather than relatively stable. To illustrate the tax effects on the value of an option on a more volatile stock, suppose that the probability a call will appreciate 300% is .2 and that the probability that it will expire unexercised is .8. Then the expected value of an option on such a volatile stock is

$$.2 \ (3) + .8 \ (-1) = -20\%$$

Given other short-term gains taxable at 70% and long-term capital gains taxable at 35%, the after-tax expected value of this option would be

$$.2 \ (3) \ (1-.35) + .8 \ (-1) \ (1-.7) = +25\%$$

In this example illustrating the case of a call on a highly volatile stock, the pre-tax expected value of the option is a negative

20%. In contrast, the post-tax expectation would be a positive value of 25%.

Thus, buyers of put and call options can clearly benefit from the peculiarities of the federal income tax laws and regulations favoring long-term capital gains, which are taxable at half the rates applicable to ordinary income. Since an option is considered a capital asset, the holder of a "worthless" 190-day option can establish a short-term capital loss by selling it to a third party for a nominal price of $1 just before the six-month holding period elapses. A profitable option can be sold to establish a long-term capital gain after the six-month holding period, instead of exercising the option. This favorable tax treatment is especially attractive for purchasing puts in preference to selling stock short, because any gain on a short sale is always deemed short-term and never a long-term capital gain.

PUTS

The tax consequences of a put purchase are delayed until the option transaction is closed. If the buyer of a put permits the option to lapse without being exercised, its expiration is deemed a sale and the cost of the option constitutes a capital loss on the expiration date. This loss is treated as short-term or long-term, depending upon the holding period of the option.

If a put option is sold, the difference between the proceeds and the cost of the option constitutes a capital gain or loss. However, if the put is exercised, the exercise of the put constitutes a sale of stock and the cost of the put option is substracted from the proceeds of the sale of the stock. The resultant capital gain or loss on the stock is treated as short-term or long-term, depending upon the holding period of the stock sold.

A put option may be bought to fix the amount of the gain on a particular stock in the current year while postponing the tax liability on the capital gain to the following year, if the investor's tax position will be more favorable the succeeding year. This can be done by purchasing a put covering the underlying shares with a contract period extending into the suceeding year, so that the profit is in effect frozen at the current market price but the gain is not established for tax purposes until the put is exercised the following year. This deferral of the tax liability does not affect the short-term or long-term nature of the capital gain on the stock, since its holding period is determined at the time of the put purchase.

The treatment of a put option as a capital asset permits an option holder to realize capital gains. For example, suppose that after the purchase of a 190-day put on U.S. Steel at $40, the price of the stock drops to $20. This profitable option must not be exercised, because the purchase of the stock at $20 and its immediate sale to the option writer would constitute a short-term profit. Instead of exercising this put privilege, this option could be sold after the six-month holding period to any third party for its market value. In this way, there may be established a long-term capital gain taxable at only half the rate of a short-term gain.

On the other hand, if the price of the stock rose, the sale of the "worthless" put option just before the end of the six-month holding period to an option dealer or any third party for a nominal price of $1 would create a short-term loss. This could be deducted from short-term gains, which are taxable at the same rate as ordinary income. If this option holder is in the 50% income tax bracket, the establishment of the short-term loss provides an out-of-pocket loss of only 50%. In contrast, if this "worthless" option had been allowed to lapse and thus be treated as a sale on the expiration date, the resulting long-term loss would have been deductible from long-term capital gains favorably taxed at only half the ordinary rate.

These examples illustrate the tax advantages of put options held longer than six months. Prior to the end of the six-month holding period, any loss on such an option may be established by

97

its sale as a short-term loss deductible from highly taxed short-term capital gains. On the other hand, any profit may be established by the sale of the option after the six-month holding period as a long-term capital gain taxable at only half the ordinary rate.

In fact, the simultaneous purchase of a put and the underlying stock could realize both a short-term loss and a long-term capital gain. To illustrate such a dual transaction, suppose that U.S. Steel is bought at $40 and at the same time a 190-day put option for this stock is purchased for a $400 premium. If the price of the stock falls to $20 just before the end of the six-month period, these shares could be sold to establish a $2,000 short-term capital loss. After the end of the six-month period, the put option could be sold for its market value to establish a long-term capital gain of $1,600.

On the other hand, if the price of the stock rose to $60 at the end of six months, the "worthless" put option could be sold for a nominal price of $1 to any third party to establish a short-term capital loss of $400. The following day the shares could be sold to realize a long-term capital gain of some $2,000 (less transaction costs).

While these general rules ordinarily can produce favorable tax consequences, a put option may be treated as a short sale resulting in unfavorable tax treatment in some situations:

SPECIAL TAX RESTRICTIONS ON PUTS

Unless a put is purchased at the same time as the underlying stock, a put purchase is generally regarded as a short sale for tax purposes if the stock is held six months or less at the time the option is bought. Hence, like a short sale, any profit on such a put purchase is fully taxable as a short-term gain, no matter how long the put option is held.[4]

This tax restriction means that if the underlying stock is held

---

[4] Section 1233 (b) of the Internal Revenue Code.

on a short-term basis when the put is purchased or that if the stock is acquired while the put is held, the holding period for the related stock does not start until the put is exercised or expires or until the option is sold.

To illustrate, suppose that a one-year put is purchased on a stock held for six months and then the option is allowed to expire unexercised. Although a year and a half has elapsed since stock was acquired, the holding period of the stock for tax purposes does not begin until the expiration date of the put option.

But there are three exceptions to these special tax restrictions on put purchases:

1. If the stock holding is already long-term when the put is purchased, any profit on the sale of the stock qualifies as a long-term capital gain (provided that such stock would actually be used if the put is exercised).

2. If both the underlying stock and the put are purchased on the same day, then the put is not treated as a short sale. If such put is allowed to expire unexercised, the cost of the option may be added to the cost of the underlying stock.

3. If the put is sold, the holding period of the underlying stock runs from the date the stock was actually acquired.[5]

Ordinarily, if a put is purchased when the holding period of the underlying stock is less than six months, the acquisition of the put constitutes a short sale and thus prevents the establishment of a long-term capital gain after six months. However, a private ruling by the Internal Revenue Service limits the applicability of this short sale rule to those situations where the put is either exercised or allowed to expire unexercised. If the put option is sold, the holding period of the shares runs from the date the stock was actually purchased.

Now if the price of the underlying stock declines, the put can be sold after six-months to establish a long-term capital gain, with-

---

[5] CPA *Journal*, "Tax Planning with CBOE Options," August 1974, p. 45.

out tainting the long-term holding period for the stock. On the other hand, if the price of the stock rises, the put can be sold before it has been held for six months to realize a short-term loss and then the underlying stock can be sold to establish a long-term capital gain. In this way, a put can be acquired to convert a short-term into a long-term capital gain on a stock.

Here is an example how a put might be utilized to protect a profit on a stock and also to convert a short-term gain into a long-term capital gain: Suppose you own 100 shares of stock purchased a month ago at 15 and the shares are selling at 25. Then a 190-day put option at 25 might be bought for a $250 premium to protect the profit on the stock. If the price of the shares should fall to 10 just after the end of the six-month holding period for the put option, the option could be sold to establish a long-term capital gain of $1,250 on the option. The stock could be sold the following day to realize a $500 long-term capital loss on the shares. Thus, the overall results on the sale of both the stock and the option would show a net long-term capital gain of $750 (before commissions).

On the other hand, had the stock advanced to 35, the option could be sold for a nominal price of $1 just before the end of the six-month holding period for the underlying stock to establish a short-term loss of $249 on the option. The following day the shares would be sold to establish a long-term capital gain of $2,000 on the stock.

OPTION WRITING

Option writers enjoy tax advantages, too. A premium received for writing an option is not included in income at the time of receipt, because it is considered deferred income for tax purposes. Premium income is deferred until the option is exercised or expires, or until the option writer engages in a closing transaction, although the option writer receives an immediate cash payment of the premium.

If the option writer buys stock pursuant to exercise of a put, the premium received by him is used to reduce the cost basis of the stock purchased. If the writer sells the underlying stock pursuant to exercise of a call, the premium received increases the amount realized upon the sale of such stock in determining his gain or loss. Such capital gain or loss is short-term or long-term, depending upon the holding period of the stock sold.

A premium received from a lapsed option generally constitutes ordinary income upon expiration. However, unlike individual puts or calls, the premium received from a lapsed option written as part of a straddle may be treated as a short-term capital gain (instead of ordinary income).[6]

If an option writer engages in a closing transaction by payment of an amount equivalent to the value of the option at the time of such payment, then the difference between the amount so paid and the premium received is ordinary income or loss. This new Internal Revenue Service ruling allows much greater tax benefits than were previously possible for option writers. A covered call writer can liquidate an "in the money" option and thereby realize an ordinary loss deductible from ordinary income while realizing a long-term capital gain on the covering stock.[7]

For example, suppose an option writer purchases XYZ stock at $40 and simultaneously sells a 190-day call for a $500 premium on the Chicago Board Options Exchange. Should the price of the stock rise to $60 after six months, the writer has the following choices:

(a) If he lets the call be exercised, the result will be a $500 long-capital gain (aside from commissions).

(b) If the writer engages in a closing purchase transaction and the option is selling at 20, he would purchase it for $2,000, sustaining an ordinary loss of $1,500. Then he would sell his

---

[6] Section 1234 (c) of the Internal Revenue Code, as amended by Section 210 (b) of the Foreign Investors Tax Act of 1966.

[7] CPA Journal, pp. 45-46.

stock for $6,000, thereby establishing a long-term capital gain of $2,000. While the $1,500 ordinary loss on the option can offset other ordinary income, only one-half of the $2,000 long-term capital gain is taxable.

If the option writer is in the 50% income tax bracket, the $1,500 ordinary loss on the option saves $750 in taxes and costs him only $750 out-of-pocket, while the $2,000 capital gain produces $1,500 after taxes. Thus, these transactions yield a net return of $750 after taxes. As an alternative, had the writer waited for the call to be exercised and simply delivered his stock to fulfill the option contract, he would have realized a long-term capital gain of $500, of which he would have retained only $375 after taxes. In effect, the net return was doubled to $750 by engaging in the closing purchase transaction, to sustain an ordinary loss on the option and then establishing the long-term capital gain on the underlying stock.

However, the exercise of an option is not within control of the writer. An unwelcome exercise notice might arrive when the holding period for the stock is still short-term. The exercise of a call becomes likely as the market price of the underlying stock rises above the exercise price of the option and as the call approaches its expiration date. Hence, an option writer should consider a closing purchase of an "in the money" call as soon as he expects the option to be exercised, so that ordinary income can be converted into a long-term capital gain.

If an unwelcome exercise notice is received while the holding period for the stock is still short-term, the writer of the covered call can immediately buy additional shares for delivery against the exercised option (resulting in a short-term capital loss on the stock) and then write a new call on the shares originally held. After the long-term holding period is established, the writer could engage in a closing purchase transaction (resulting in an ordinary loss) and sell the appreciated stock (realizing a long-term capital gain).

102

It is very important that the exercise of the unwelcome call not result in a short sale, in order to protect the long-term capital gain possibility. If the shares delivered against the exercised call are not owned by the writer, the call would result in a short sale, thus tainting the holding period of the stock already owned. On account of the six-day settlement required on exercised options, this possible problem can be prevented by purchasing the additional shares for regular five-day delivery as soon as the unwelcome exercise notice is received.

It is also very important that the securities delivered to establish the short-term gain be adequately identified in order to assure desired tax consequences. Where various lots of a security are acquired at different times or at different prices, and only a part of the holding is sold, the investor must specify to the broker the particular securities to be sold at the time of the sale. The identification should show purchase date and cost. Written confirmation must be received from the broker within a reasonable period of time thereafter. The first-in first-out rule would apply if the securities sold are not adequately identified.

STRADDLES

For federal income tax purposes, the term "straddle means a simultaneously granted combination of an option to buy, and an option to sell, the same quantity of a security at the same price during the same period of time."[8]

The premium received for writing a straddle must be allocated between the constituent put and call options on the basis of the relative market value of such component options at the time the straddle was written or on any other reasonable and consistent basis acceptable to the Internal Revenue Service. In lieu of respective market values, the straddle writer may elect to allocate 55% of the premium to the call and 45% to the put option. For

---

[8] Section 1234 (c) of the Internal Revenue Code.

example, if a writer receives a $2,000 premium on the sale of a straddle, he may allocate $1,100 to the call and $900 to the put option.

The premium allocated to an exercised put is used to reduce the cost of the stock acquired and the premium allocated to an exercised call is added to the proceeds of the sale of the stock sold. The income from a lapsed part of a straddle is deemed a short-term capital gain. If the option writer engages in a closing transaction by payment of an amount equivalent to the value of the option at the time of such payment, the difference between the amount so paid and the premium received is ordinary income or loss.

To illustrate the tax consequences for a straddle writer, suppose ABC stock is bought for $80 per share and a 190-day straddle at an option price of $80 is sold simultaneously for a $2,000 premium. If the price of the stock should fall from $80 to $60 by the end of the contract period, the shares would be put to the writer at the $80 exercise price. The cost of the acquired stock for tax purposes is reduced by $900, the value allocated to the put side of the straddle, so that the per share cost is $71 rather than $80. The $1,100 portion of the premium attributed to the unexercised call side of the straddle is deemed a short-term capital gain. Should the writer want to dispose of his original holding as well as the newly acquired stock, he is now in a position to write calls on 200 shares and thus receive additional premiums amounting to some $1,500. In this way, the shares might be sold above the current market price or their cost will be further reduced.

On the other hand, if the price of the stock rises from $80 to $100 at the end of the contract period, the put side of the straddle will lapse and the $900 portion of the premium allocated to the unexercised put is deemed a short-term capital gain. Instead of allowing the call to be exercised, the writer could engage in a closing transaction by purchasing the call option for $2,000, thus sustaining an ordinary loss of $900 ($2,000 —$1,100 premium). Then the underlying stock would be sold for $10,000, thereby establishing a long-term capital gain of $2,000 ($10,000 —$8,000 cost).

If the option writer is in the 50% income tax bracket, the ordinary loss saves $450 in taxes and thus costs him only $450 out-of-pocket, while the short-term gain yields $450 after taxes and the long-term capital gain yields $1,500 after taxes. Thus, these transactions would produce a net return of $1,500 after taxes (ignoring commissions).

TAX-EXEMPT INSTITUTIONS

A financial institution should first ascertain the position of its supervisory authority before dealing in options, since its tax status may depend upon approved guidelines set by government regulations.

Premiums from unexercised options could be construed by the Internal Revenue Service as taxable "unrelated business income" to an otherwise tax-exempt institution.[9] However, the premium from the lapsed part of a straddle is deemed a short-term capital gain rather than ordinary income.[10] Capital gains as well as dividends, interest and annuities are excluded from income in arriving at taxable "unrelated business income."[11]

The Comptroller of the Currency has authorized national banks to write call options on securities held in trust accounts, where specific authority for such transactions is contained in the governing trust instrument. Among others, the Illinois Insurance Department has sanctioned both writing and limited buying of listed options. The New York Insurance Superintendent has permitted insurers to write covered call options traded on a securities ex-

---

[9] Section 512 of the Internal Revenue Code.
[10] Section 1234 (c) of the Internal Revenue Code, as amended by Section 210 (b) of the Foreign Investors Tax Act of 1966.
[11] Section 512 of the Internal Revenue Code.

change and to purchase call options to close out prior option trans-actions. The States of Tennessee and Connecticut have allowed their employee pension funds to deal in options.

The purchase of options or the writing of "naked" or uncovered calls could jeopardize the tax-exempt status of a philanthropic foundation and could result in imposition of heavy excise taxes.

INVESTMENT COMPANIES

Distributed income of a regulated investment company or-dinarily is not subject to federal income taxes, but this tax treat-ment may be denied if more than 10% of total income is received from sources other than dividends, interest and capital gains.[12] Since premium income from unexercised options could be con-strued as part of this 10% limit, option writing must be carefully limited by regulated investment companies.

PERSONAL HOLDING COMPANIES

Option writing "income could help keep a corporation out of reach of the personal holding company tax."[13]

A closely held corporation (over 50% owned by fewer than six people) becomes a personal holding company subject to the 70% tax on undistributed earnings when at least 60% of its "adjusted ordinary gross income" consists of "personal holding company income" including dividends, interest, rent and royal-ties.[14] All capital gains and losses are excluded from personal holding company income and from adjusted ordinary gross in-come, so that any capital gains resulting from option writing play no role in the determination of holding company status. While premium income from unexercised options is included in adjusted

---

[12] Section 851 (b) of the Internal Revenue Code.

[13] Oppenheim, Appel, Dixon & Co., *Tax Considerations in Using CBOE Options* (Chicago: Chicago Board Option Exchange, 1975), p. 16.

[14] Sections 541 and 542 of the Internal Revenue Code.

ordinary gross income, it is excluded from personal holding company income.

Thus, through the receipt of sufficient premiums from option writing, less than 60% of adjusted ordinary gross income would be derived from personal holding company income. In this way, a closely held corporation could completely avoid the personal holding company tax.

CHAPTER 7

Chicago Board Options Exchange

The birth of the Chicago Board Options Exchange on April 26, 1973, ushered in a bright new era in options trading. As the world's first organized securities exchange dealing solely in options, it provides a continuous auction market in standardized option contracts. This Exchange permits both writers and holders to originate options as well as to liquidate their positions through offsetting transactions.

OVER-THE-COUNTER OPTIONS MARKET

In the United States prior to the organization of the Chicago Board Options Exchange, there was no central market place for options so that puts and calls were traded solely in the over-the-counter options market. Brokers and dealers, trying to match individual buy and sell orders, were often unable to find either a buyer or an option writer willing to deal in any option on a particular security. The negotiating process of bringing an option writer and buyer together was cumbersome and relatively inefficient. No continuous auction market in option contracts existed.

There was virtually no effective secondary market, because practically every individual option contract written was different. Both the exercise price and the expiration date varied in each contract. Consequently, neither option holders nor writers could easily liquidate their positions through offsetting transactions before the contracts expired, so that an option holder and the writer were virtually linked together for the duration of the option.

TABLE XIII

Total Volume of Options in the Over-the-Counter Market
(thousands of shares)

1937—1973

Year	Volume	Ratio to N.Y.S.E. Volume
1937	2,246	.55%
1938	1,423	.48
1939	1,142	.44
1940	1,205	.58
1941	835	.49
1942	685	.55
1943	1,371	.49
1944	1,691	.64
1945	2,108	.56
1946	1,698	.47
1947	1,218	.48
1948	1,664	.55
1949	1,382	.51
1950	2,631	.50
1951	3,279	.74
1952	3,102	.92
1953	2,663	.75
1954	4,070	.71
1955	6,012	.93

TABLE XIII (continued)

Year	Volume	Ratio to N.Y.S.E. Volume
1956	5,559	1.00
1957	5,396	.96
1958	6,485	.87
1959	8,842	1.08
1960	8,561	1.12
1961	13,322	1.30
1962	7,842	.82
1963	9,630	.84
1964	11,019	.90
1965	15,257	.98
1966	15,189	.80
1967	23,811	.94
1968	30,285	1.05
1969	28,265	1.03
1970	19,681	.67
1971	29,516	.76
1972	32,851	.79
1973	18,920	.47

Sources: Put and Call Brokers and Dealers Association and the New York Stock Exchange.

Detailed or systematic reporting on bids and offers and actual prices was clearly lacking. It was very difficult for a buyer or a seller to know what a fair market price was. In fact, during the negotiations with the options dealer, neither the buyer nor the writer knew whether there was any active participant on the other side of the market or whether the dealer was merely shopping for a possible trade. As a result, most investors refused to deal in the over-the-counter options market.

Despite the extreme difficulties encountered in trading options in the over-the-counter market, the volume expanded with total trading in common stocks. Since the 1930's, the volume of trading in puts and calls in the over-the-counter options market grew along with the total volume of transactions in stocks on the New York Stock Exchange.

The volume of trading in options also increased in relation to total stock market activity. In the fourteen years 1960 through 1973, option sales amounted to almost 1% of New York Stock Exchange sales, compared with hardly more than one-half of 1% in the same number of earlier years 1937 through 1950. Trading of puts and calls in the over-the-counter options market, however, was more volatile than total stock market activity. Volume in the option market tended to be relatively larger when stock prices were generally rising and to decline relative to New York Stock Exchange activity in periods of declining stock prices. When stock prices fell, disappointed option buyers usually withdrew from the market and many regular writers expecting a rebound in stock prices were unwilling to sell calls related to the reduced price level.

CHICAGO BOARD OPTIONS EXCHANGE

In the face of the 1973 decline in the stock market along with the drop in conventional option trading activity in the over-the-counter market, the volume of transactions on the newly organized Chicago Board Options Exchange boomed. Shortly after it opened, the average daily volume in call option contracts covering about 100,000 shares on a pilot list of only 16 stocks exceeded the combined total of all other activity in puts, calls and other types of options on all stocks. By 1975, activity had multiplied some fifty-fold to a daily volume of options on 5,000,000 shares, though listings were limtied to only 40 stocks. In terms of aggregate share volume, the Chicago Board Options Exchange had become the second largest securities exchange in the United States. Measured in terms of volume per stock listed, the CBOE had far surpassed the New York Stock Exchange, too.

This upsurge in option trading activity should continue for a variety of reasons. The Chicago Board Options Exchange, which at present trades in calls on only 40 common stocks, plans to double the number to 80 by 1976. The CBOE also intends to add trading in puts as well as the calls now traded. These additions could double the total volume of option trading.

As the world's first securities exchange established for the prime purpose of providing an organized options market, the Chicago Board Options Exchange represents a vast improvement over the traditional means of dealing in options by surmounting the distinct disadvantages experienced in the over-the-counter options market. An organized market in standardized option contracts brings numerous and considerable advantages:

1. Standarization of terms
2. Severance of buyer-writer tie
3. Secondary market
4. Dividend retention

5. Narrowing spread
6. Commission savings
7. Tax savings
8. Market liquidity

STANDARDIZATION OF TERMS

Unlike conventional options traded in the over-the-counter market, Chicago Board Options have standardized expiration dates and exercise prices, leaving option prices as the only variable determined by trading in the auction market.

A listed option expires at 4:00 P.M. Central Time, 5:00 P.M. Eastern Time, on the Saturday immediately following the third Friday of the expiration month. Trading in options of a particular expiration month normally begins nine months earlier and options having at least three different expiration months are generally open for trading.

Exercise prices are generally fixed at 5 point intervals for stocks trading below 50; 10 point intervals for stocks trading between 50 and 100; 20 point intervals for stocks trading between 100 and 200; and 25 point intervals for stocks trading above 200. When

113

trading is initiated in a new expiration month, the Exchange ordinarily selects the exercise price closest to the market price of the underlying stock. For example, if the underlying stock sells at 17 when trading is introduced in a new expiration month, the exercise price will ordinarily be fixed at 15.

When significant price movements occur in an underlying stock following the introduction of new expiration months, additional options with exercise prices reflecting such price movements may be opened for trading for one or more of the expiration months already the subject of trading. If the price of the underlying stock has moved very rapidly, two new exercise prices may be opened at the same time.

Once trading in an option is initiated, it remains open for trading until 2 P.M. Central Time of the last business day immediately prior to the expiration date, unless trading is suspended or limited by the Exchange in the interest of a fair and orderly market. For instance, opening transactions are now prohibited where the exercise price is more than $5 above the closing price of the underlying stock and the option price less than 50¢ on the last day traded. Not included in these prohibitions are opening sales transactions of covered call options or any closing transactions.

SEVERANCE OF BUYER-WRITER TIE

In the over-the-counter options market, the buyer and writer remain linked during the life of the option contract. Whenever a listed option is issued to a holder, there is a writer of an option having the same terms contractually obligated to the Options Clearing Corporation an account of that option. The holder of the option, however, does not look to any particular writer for performance. Instead, the Options Clearing Corporation is the issuer and obligor on every outstanding listed option. Its aggregate obligations to holders of options are backed up by the aggregate contractual obligations which writers owe to the Options Clearing

114

Corporation. When an option is exercised, the Clearing Corporation assigns an exercise notice to a Clearing Member randomly selected from among those having an account with the same terms as the exercised option. The selected Clearing Member is obligated to deliver the underlying stock against payment of the exercise price. In this way, the option buyer-writer tie is virtually severed.

SECONDARY MARKET

The combination of standardization of contract terms and unlinking of specific holders and writers facilitates a continuous secondary market, in which an existing position of a holder or writer may be liquidated by an offsetting closing transaction. Such secondary market permits a holder of an Exchange Traded Option to realize its market value by disposing of the option by a "closing sales transaction." Similarly, such secondary securities market enables the writer of an Exchange Traded Option to terminate his contractual obligation by engaging in a "closing purchase transaction."

A closing sales transaction may be illustrated by the following example: Suppose a holder had purchased an XYZ July 50 Option in January for $600 when the underlying stock was selling at 51. Three months later, the stock sells at 57 and the option at 9. In this case, the holder could realize the $300 gain in the option price (less commissions) in a "closing sale transaction." The option holder can thus liquidate his position in the secondary market, by selling an option having the same terms as the option previously purchased.

The existence of a secondary market also permits an option writer to terminate his obligation by a "closing purchase transaction," by buying an option having the same terms as the option previously written. For example, suppose a holder of XYZ stock wrote an XYZ July 50 Option in January for $600 when the stock was selling at 51. Three months later when the stock sells at 45 and the option at 2, the writer anticipates a further decline

115

in the price of the stock. Since his option still has three months to run, the sale of his stock to eliminate any further loss would place him in the position of a "naked" writer and thus clearly expose him to unlimited upside risk if the price of the stock should rise. To avoid this "naked" risk, the writer could engage in a "closing purchase transaction," paying $200 plus transaction costs. This closes out his writer's option position, leaving him free to sell his underlying stock.

DIVIDEND RETENTION

Unlike conventional options traded in the over-the-counter market, no adjustment is made to any of the terms of Exchange Traded Options to reflect the declaration or payment of ordinary cash dividends. However, if a holder files an effective exercise notice with the Options Clearing Corporation prior to an ex-dividend date the exercising holder is entitled to that dividend even though the writer to whom the exercise is assigned may receive actual notice of such assignment after the ex-dividend date.

Adjustments to the terms of Exchange Traded Options are effective as of the "ex-date" of the event giving rise to the adjustment. Stock splits and other stock distributions, which increase the number of outstanding shares of the issuer of the underlying stock, have the effect of proportionately increasing the number of shares of underlying stock covered by the option and decreasing the exercise price. However, where a stock split or distribution results in the issuance of whole shares of underlying stock, the number of shares covered by the option is not adjusted. Instead, the number of outstanding options is proportionately increased and the exercise price is proportionately decreased. This may be illustrated by comparing the adjustments to a single option covering 100 shares of stock at an exercise price of 60 resulting from a 3 for 2 stock distribution and a 2 for 1 stock split. After adjustment in the former case, the option covers 150 shares at an ex-

116

ercise price of 40; after adjustment in the latter case, there are two options covering 100 shares each at an exercise price of 30.

Since ordinary cash dividends on the underlying stock of Exchange Traded Options are retained by option writers, listed call options generally are less valuable to holders than comparable options traded in the over-the-counter market. However, the option writers benefit from the retention of dividends on the underlying stock of Exchange Traded Options.

NARROWING SPREAD

Compared with the cumbersome and costly over-the-counter option market, transactions in Exchange Traded Options are much more efficient and less expensive. The expedited transactions process in a continuous auction market narrows the spread between what option purchasers pay and what writers receive. An organized options exchange brings buyers and sellers together without an intervening dealer's spread, thereby effecting a reduction in transaction costs.

COMMISSION SAVINGS

Additional savings in transaction costs can be realized through a reduction in brokerage commissions involved in exercising options. An option holder who exercises a call must pay a brokerage commission to buy the stock and then another commission to sell the shares. An Exchange Traded Option, however, can easily be liquidated without either buying or selling the underlying stock, so that the total transaction costs are reduced considerably. Brokerage commissions are computed on the price of the option—not on the value of the underlying shares.

TAX SAVINGS

The existence of a secondary market for Exchange Traded Options facilitates tax savings for option writers. An "in the money"

117

covered call can be liquidated by the option writer through an offsetting "closing purchase transaction," in order to record an ordinary income loss deductible from ordinary income for tax purposes, while realizing a long-term capital gain on the underlying stock.

Suppose a writer purchases 100 shares of ABC stock at $50 and simultaneously sells a call at $50 for a $600 premium. If the price of the stock rises to $60 just before the expiration of the 190-day option period, the option writer can engage in a "closing purchase transaction," by buying an option having the same terms as the option previously written. Should the call be priced at 10, it would be bought for $1,000, sustaining an ordinary loss of $400 on the option transaction. Then the shares would be sold for $6,000, realizing a $1,000 long-term capital gain.

Had this writer allowed the option to be exercised, the tax result would have been a long-term capital gain of $600 (instead of the $1,000 long-term capital gain and the $400 ordinary loss deductible from ordinary income).

MARKET LIQUIDITY

The development of the Chicago Board Options Exchange as an organized options market practically makes a CBOE call a full-fledged security like a short-term warrant. At any time during the life of an option, both the holder and writer are free to liquidate their positions through closing offsetting transactions on the Chicago Board Options Exchange. This market liquidity reduces the risk for both the option holder and writer.

Prior to the organization of the Chicago Board Options Exchange, the option writer was contractually tied to the option holder for the life of the option. While the call writer was committed to sell his stock at any time to the option holder, he could not voluntarily liquidate his position. Furthermore, option writing on most stocks was a fickle affair seldom sustained by continuing

118

demand for calls on the same stock. Now an investor holding a CBOE—listed stock can continue to write calls, or terminate his position by repurchasing the call.

Similarly, while the holder of a traditional over-the-counter option could only exercise or not exercise his option, the holder of a CBOE call can sell his option in the secondary market at any time during the life of the option contract. The importance of the market liquidity provided by the Chicago Board Options Exchange as a secondary market in options is illustrated by the following example:

Suppose when a stock sells at $100 per share, a six-month CBOE call at the same price is purchased at a price of 12. Also suppose that a month later, this stock sells at $108 and the option is priced at 16, showing a 4 point or 33% profit on the option on an 8% gain in the underlying stock. This profit can be realized by simply selling the option on the Chicago Board Options Exchange.

In contrast, the holder of a traditional over-the-counter call under similar circumstances could not realize any profit on the 8 point advance in the price of the stock, since no organized resale or secondary market in over-the-counter options exists. Upon exercise of the over-the-counter call, this option holder would realize a 4 point loss (before commissions), because the 8 point rise in the price of the stock does not even offset the 12 point premium paid for the option. This 4 point loss on the over-the-counter call clearly contracts with the 4 point profit on the CBOE call under similar circumstances. This 8 point difference in the return between an over-the-counter and a CBOE call is solely the result of the availability of a resale or secondary option market such as the Chicago Board Options Exchange.

The greater market liquidity of listed options expands the usefulness of options for both buyers and writers, who are now free to change their positions whenever deemed desirable. An option position can be liquidated efficiently and economically by either

119

the holder or the writer at any time prior to the expiration of the contract. All participants in a listed options market may benefit from full and fast public reporting of bids and offers, actual transaction prices and the volume of trading activity. In fact, the huge trading activity on the Chicago Board Options Exchange enables financial institutions to write options in volume against their investment portfolios.

The most significant achievement of the Chicago Board Options Exchange is the development of a liquid secondary market, which enables an option holder or writer to close out a position prior to the expiration date.

CHAPTER 8

Listed Option Strategy

Unlike conventional options traded in the over-the-counter market, the exercise price of a listed option seldom coincides precisely with the market price of the underlying stock. Therefore, any strategy utilized in buying or selling listed options must take into account the effect of an "away from the market" transaction on option value.

"AWAY FROM THE MARKET"

An option is said to be trading or selling "away from the market," when the exercise price of the option differs from the market price of the underlying stock. If the exercise or striking price on an option is "away from the market," the option must be either "in the money" or "out of the money." An option is "in the

121

money" when the market price of the underlying stock is higher than the exercise price for a call or lower than the exercise price for a put. An option is "out of the money" when the market price of the underlying stock is lower than the exercise price for a call or higher than the exercise price for a put.

An option "in the money" tends to sell a a higher price than an option "out of the money," simply because an option "in the money" has a positive intrinsic value whereas an "out of the money" option has a negative intrinsic value. The excess of the market price of the underlying stock over the exercise price of the option represents the intrinsic value of a call, while the excess of the exercise price over the market price of the underlying stock represents the intrinsic value of a put.

Options ordinarily sell at premiums over their intrinsic values. Prior to expiration of an option contract, the price of an option cannot be less than it intrinsic value. For instance, suppose the striking price of an option is $50 and the price of the underlying stock is $60, the price of the option must be at least $10. Otherwise, if the option price were under $10, the stock could be bought for less than $60 by buying the option and exercising. Hence, an option cannot sell for less than its intrinsic value, except momentarily.

The exact value of an option will be known when the option contract expires. If the price of the underlying stock exceeds the exercise price of call, this difference or intrinsic value will be the price of the option. If the exercise price of the option exceeds the price of the underlying stock, the call will have a zero value.

During the life of an option contract, the premium over the intrinsic value of an option tends to be at a maximum when the exercise price of the option equals the market price of the underlying stock. The amount of the premium generally diminishes as the market price of the underlying stock moves away from the striking price of the option—in either direction.

122

Any movement in the price of the underlying stock affects the option premium, since the price of an option depends upon the market price of the underlying stock relative to the exercise price of the option. But the effect of any change in the underlying stock on the option premium is different depending upon the extent of the price movement and the direction "in the money" or "out of the money."

"IN THE MONEY"

A change in the price of an option depends upon the change in the price of the underlying stock, but such changes are not in direct proportion. As the market price of the underlying stock approaches the exercise price of the option, changes in the option price become larger and larger, until the stock price equals the striking price, when the premium value of the option tends to reach its highest level. As the stock price moves above the strik-ing price, the option price moves almost dollar for dollar with the price of the stock. As the intrinsic value of the option increases further with higher prices of the underlying stock, the premium over the intrinsic value tends to approach zero.

In other words, as the intrinsic value of an option increases, the premium tends to diminish. To illustrate, consider a call at $20 on a stock selling at that price and the option at $3. Suppose that later the same day, such stock sells at $22 so that the call is now $2 "in the money." Then would the call be worth $5 (the $3 pre-mium plus the $2 intrinsic value)? The answer is an unqualified NO! In order to realize the $2 intrinsic value, the option holder must exercise the call and thereby surrender the option value of its remaining life. Exercising this call, in fact, would produce a net loss on the option, since the $2 intrinsic value is actually less than the $3 purchase price of the option. Potential call buyers would be unwilling to pay a $5 price for this option, inasmuch as the $2 "in the money" increases both the required capital outlay

123

and the risk involved in holding the option at a higher price, which reduces the leverage.

In this example, the call is likely to be priced at about $4 (a $2 premium plus the $2 intrinsic value). The $1 net gain in the option value would thus reflect the $2 increment in intrinsic value less a $1 loss in premium value. Evidently, an advance in the price of the underlying stock increases the intrinsic value of the call as well as the total option value, but reduces the premium over the intrinsic value.

Rising option prices result in reduced leverage. As the intrinsic value of an option increases, the premium tends to decline, because the option's effective leverage diminishes. In this instance, when the price of the underlying stock was $20 and the option $3, the price of the stock was nearly 7 times that of the option. After the advance in the price of the stock, however, the stock was only 5½ times the option value. Hence, rising market prices curtail a call's leverage on the upside, but raise the risk on the downside. At higher prices, the option holder must risk larger capital outlays as against less leverage.

The resulting decline in the premium over the intrinsic value makes writing "in the money" options less attractive, too. Whenever the price of the underlying stock rises rapidly after the sale of a call, the writer could consider switching his option position by engaging in a closing purchase transaction and simultaneously selling an "out of the money" call at a higher exercise price for a larger premium. The premium on an "in the money" option is generally smaller than that on an "out of the money" option.

To illustrate, suppose a covered writer sells a six-month call at $100 on a stock selling at that price for a $15 premium. Should the stock rise to $120 within three months and the call is priced at only its $20 intrinsic value, this option could be repurchased and the shares sold to realize the $15 maximum profit potential in only half the time ($20 gain on the stock less the $5 loss on the

124

option). Or the shares could be retained and another call at a higher exercise price sold at a premium.

"OUT OF THE MONEY"

When the market price of the underlying stock slips to the level of the exercise price, the intrinsic option value is zero and the call is "out of the money." As the price of the stock falls below the exercise price, the option premium also decreases, but the option price changes less than dollar for dollar with the price of the underlying stock. In a declining market, the premium of an "out of the money" call tends to diminish at a decreasing rate.

Declining market prices result in increasing leverage, which makes calls more attractive to option holders. Although the option price changes less than the price of the underlying stock in absolute terms, percentage changes in the price of the option will tend to be greater than the percentage changes in the price of the under-lying stock. For instance, consider the call at $20 when the market price of the stock was $22 and the option $4. Should the price of the stock fall from $22 to $15, the option value would decline from $4 to about $1. Consequently, the stock would be selling at 15 times the value of the option. Clearly, a price decline reduces a call's relative risk on the downside, but raises the lever-age on the upside.

The premium on an "out of the money" option is generally greater than that on an "in the money" option, because an "in the money" option contains both an intrinsic value and a premium value whereas an "out of the money" option has no intrinsic value to be deducted from the total option value. The intrinsic value is a factor only in the case of an option "in the money," when the market price of the underlying stock exceeds the ex-ercise price. The premium value tends to be at a maximum when the market price equals the exercise price. The premium tends to diminish, as the market price of the underlying stock moves away from the option's exercise price.

As the market price of the underlying stock moves below the exercise price, the intrinsic value is zero and the premium value tends to decline. On the other hand, as the market price moves above the exercise price, the intrinsic value increases, but the premium over the intrinsic value tends to approach zero and then the option price tends to move dollar for dollar with the price of the underlying stock.

Should the price of the underlying stock fall precipitously after the sale of a call, the writer could consider engaging in a closing purchase transaction to realize his profit on the option position. The possible remaining return on the option must be compared with available premiums on alternative options. If a much more attractive option on the same security offers a significantly larger premium, then a switch may be in order.

DIVIDENDS

Unlike options traded in the over-the-counter market, the holder of a listed call is not entitled to receive ordinary cash dividends declared or paid during the life of the option contract. Since the price of the underlying stock is likely to fall by the amount of the dividend on an ex-dividend date, a listed call option on a dividend yielding stock cannot be worth as much as an option on the same stock if it were not paying a dividend. For this reason, expected dividends during the life of the option contract are subtracted from the market price of the underlying stock to estimate the option value.

Here is a simple formula for the premium percentage on a listed call option, taking into account the discounted value of expected dividends during the life of the option contract:

$$\text{Premium} = \frac{\text{option price} - \text{intrinsic value}}{\text{price of stock} - \text{option price} - \text{dividends}}$$

To illustrate, suppose a $6 option price is paid for a CBOE call at 20 for a stock selling at $22 and the discounted value of the expected dividends is $1. In this example, the $2 spread between the $22 market price and the $20 exercise price is the intrinsic value of the option and the $4 excess of the $6 option price over its $2 intrinsic value represents the option premium. Here is how the formula for the premium percentage on this listed call option is calculated:

$$\text{Premium} = \frac{6-2}{22-6-1} = 26.7\%$$

Here is a formula for the maximum potential return to the writer of a covered call on a stock selling below the exercise price of the option:

$$\text{Maximum return} = \frac{\text{option price} + \text{exercise price} - \text{price of stock}}{\text{price of stock} - \text{option price} - \text{dividends}}$$

To illustrate, suppose a $3 option price is received for a CBOE call at 25 for a stock selling at 20 and the value of the expected dividends is $1. Here is how the formula for the maximum potential return to the covered call writer would be calculated:

$$\text{Maximum return} = \frac{3+25-20}{20-3-1} = 50\%$$

Since the value of an option varies with the duration of the contract, the premium over the intrinsic value of an option decreases as the remaining life of the option diminishes with the passage of time. Accordingly, when writing covered calls, the following minimum premium percentages might be employed to take into account the remaining life of the option:

127

TABLE XIV

Expected Premium Percentages on Listed Options

Remaining Months	Premium Percentage
1	5
2	6
3	7
4	8
5	9
6	10
7	11
8	12
9	13

VOLATILITY

These expected premium percentages must be adjusted for differences in volatility of the underlying stocks, because the value of an option increases with the expected variance in the price of the underlying stock.[1] Wide swings in the price of a stock tend to be followed by wide fluctuations, though not necessarily in the same directions.[2]

Total variance or risk consists of risk due to a stock's own inherent volatility and the risk due to the general market. The Alpha factor or the risk peculiar to individual securities can be eliminated through diversification. The Beta factor or the systematic risk associated with fluctuations in the general market averages cannot

---

[1] Burton G. Malkiel and Richard E. Quandt, *Strategies and Rational Decisions in the Security Option Market* (Cambridge, Mass.: M.I.T. Press, 1969), pp. 27-31.

[2] Eugene F. Fama, "The Behavior of Stock Market Prices," *Journal of Business*, Jan. 1965, p. 87.

be eliminated through diversification, because this systematic risk is common to all stocks.[3]

The expected premium percentages are adjusted for the Beta coefficients of the underlying stocks, since covered call writers may expect to be compensated for the variability or risk involved in holding such securities. For example, if the expected premium percentage of a call on a typical stock with a remaining option life of six months is 10%, then the expected premium percentage on a stock with a 1.5 Beta coefficient would be 15%.

QUALITY OR SAFETY

The quality of a security or its safety rating reflects the total risk of holding the particular security, including the stock's inherent volatility plus its sensitivity to fluctuations in the general market averages. This total risk is measured by the volatility or total variance of the stock's price fluctuations. The riskier stocks experience more volatile or wider fluctuations than the higher quality or safer securities.

Average rates of return on common stocks generally rise with risk, but at a decelerating rate. The top quality in the first quintile containing the stocks with the least variable returns has a smaller rate of return than the stocks in the second quintile, which generally has a smaller rate of return than the average stocks in the third quintile, which in turn has a smaller return than the below average stocks in the fourth quintile. But the average rate of return for the lowest quality stocks in the fifth quintile with the greatest volatility is typically lower than for higher quality stocks.[4]

---

[3] William F. Sharpe, *Portfolio Theory and Capital Markets* (New York: McGraw-Mill, 1970), p. 97 and Frank B. Campanella, *The Measurement of Portfolio Risk Exposure: Use of the Beta Coefficient* (Lexington, Mass.: D. C. Heath, 1972), pp. 11-14.

[4] Shannon Pratt, "Relationships Between Risk and Rate of Return for Common Stock" (Indiana University dissertation, 1966) in James H. Lorie and Mary T. Hamilton, *The Stock Market: Theories and Evidence* (Homewood, Ill.: Richard D. Irwin, 1973), pp. 215-226.

Since the average rates of return on common stocks increase with risk at a decelerating rate, risk premiums are not strictly proportional to their Beta coefficients. Returns on stocks with high Betas are lower than expected on the basis of risk, because there is an inverse relationship between Alpha and Beta coefficients. Hence, top quality stocks with low Betas are more rewarding than lowest quality stocks with high Beta coefficients.[5]

A quality — highest

B quality — above average

C quality — average

D quality — below average

E quality — lowest

Based largely on past experience, these quality or safety ratings are not static and can vary in the future. Nonetheless, option writers must carefully avoid the lowest quality securities, since such stocks are too risky to hold in an investment portfolio under any circumstances and their typical return is lower than for stocks of higher quality. A below-average quality stock may be carefully considered as an exception if the percentage premium promises to provide compensation in excess of the above-average risk involved. An average quality stock may be considered only if the percentage premium promises an above-average return. An above-average quality stock may be favored if the percentage premium promises to compensate for its Beta factor. Since the highest quality stocks are the relatively least volatile, somewhat below-average percentage premiums may be acceptable on such safe securities. On the other hand, option buyers favor the lowest quality stocks since such securities are the most volatile and hence promise the greatest leverage to option holders.

---

[5] Fischer Black, Michael Jensen and Myron S. Scholes, "The Capital Asset Pricing Model: Some Empirical Tests" in Michael C. Jensen, ed. *Studies in the Theory of Capital Markets* (New York: Praeger, 1972).

TABLE XV

Volatility and Safety Ratings of Chicago Board Options

Common Stock	Beta Coefficient	Quality
Alcoa	1.05	C
American Telephone	.75	A
Atlantic Richfield	1.10	C
Avon Products	1.20	B
Bethlehem Steel	1.05	B
Brunswick	1.75	D
Citicorp	1.25	A
Delta Air Lines	1.45	C
Dow Chemical	1.10	A
Eastman Kodak	1.05	A
Exxon	.95	A
Federal National Mortgage	1.25	D
Ford Motor	1.00	B
General Electric	1.05	A
General Motors	1.00	A
Great Western Financial	1.65	D
Gulf & Western	1.35	C
IBM	1.05	B
INA	1.10	C
International Harvester	1.05	B
International Paper	1.05	B
International Telephone	1.20	C
Kennecott Copper	1.00	C
Kerr-McGee	1.05	B
Kresge	1.25	C
Loews	1.55	D
McDonald's	1.55	C
Merck	1.05	B
Minnesota Mining	1.05	B
Monsanto	1.15	B
Northwest Airlines	1.65	C
Pennzoil	1.35	C
Polaroid	1.45	C
RCA	1.20	C
Sears Roebuck	1.00	A
Sperry Rand	1.30	C
Texas Instruments	1.35	C
Upjohn	1.10	C
Weyerhaeuser	1.05	C
Xerox	1.20	B

131

TABLE XVI

Volatility and Safety Ratings of Proposed Chicago Board Options

Common Stock	Beta Coefficient	Quality
American Electric Power	.85	B
American Hospital Supply	1.25	C
Baxter Laboratories	1.10	C
Black & Decker	1.20	B
Boeing	1.25	C
Boise Cascade	1.35	C
CBS	1.15	C
Coca-Cola	1.10	A
Colgate-Palmolive	1.10	B
Commonwealth Edison	.80	B
Control Data	1.55	D
General Dynamics	1.40	D
General Foods	.90	B
Halliburton	1.10	C
Hewlett-Packard	1.30	C
Holiday Inns	1.50	C
Homestake Mining	1.30	C
Honeywell	1.15	C
International Minerals	1.30	D
Jim Walter	1.35	C
Johns-Manville	1.00	C
Johnson & Johnson	.95	B
Mobil Oil	.95	B
NCR	1.30	C
Occidental Petroleum	1.10	E
Raytheon	1.25	C
Reynolds Industries	.95	B
Schlumberger	1.10	C
Skyline	1.45	D
SONY	1.05	C
Standard Oil Indiana	.85	B
Syntex	1.30	D
Tesero Petroleum	1.35	D
Texasgulf	1.10	C
UAL	1.55	D
United Technologies	1.00	C
Utah International	1.00	C

TABLE XVII

Volatility and Safety Ratings of American Exchange Options

Common Stock	Beta Coefficient	Quality
Aetna Life Insurance	1.15	C
American Cyanamid	1.00	B
American Home	1.10	A
AMF	1.30	C
ASA	1.30	C
Beatrice Foods	1.00	B
Burroughs	1.40	C
Caterpillar Tractor	1.15	B
Chase Manhattan	.95	B
Deere	1.25	C
Digital Equipment	1.35	C
Disney	1.40	C
Du Pont	.95	A
First Charter Financial	1.45	D
General Telephone	1.05	B
Gillette	1.05	C
Goodyear	1.10	B
Grace	1.05	B
Greyhound	.80	B
Gulf Oil	.90	B
Hercules	.95	B
Merrill Lynch	1.35	C
Mesa Petroleum	1.30	C
Motorola	1.35	C
Pfizer	1.20	B
Phelps Dodge	.90	C
Philip Morris	1.15	B
Phillips Petroleum	1.10	C
Proctor & Gamble	1.00	A
Searle	1.10	C
Standard Oil California	1.05	B
Sterling Drug	1.05	B
Tenneco	.90	B
Texaco	.95	B
Tiger International	1.65	D
Union Carbide	1.15	B
U.S. Steel	1.00	B
Warner-Lambert	1.20	B
Westinghouse	1.05	B
Zenith Radio	1.35	C

TABLE XVIII

Volatility and Safety Ratings of Proposed
American Exchange Options

Common Stock	Beta Coefficient	Quality
Beneficial	1.05	B
British Petroleum	.80	C
Communications Satellite	1.10	C
Continental Telephone	.95	B
El Paso	.90	C
GAF	1.25	C
International Flavors	1.35	B
International Nickel	.90	B
Louisiana Pacific	1.60	D
McDonnell Douglas	1.20	D
MGIC	1.90	C
National Semiconductor	1.75	E
Pitney Bowes	1.20	C
Royal Dutch Petroleum	.70	B
Santa Fe	1.00	C
Scott Paper	1.10	C
Signal	1.05	C
Southern California Edison	.85	B
Simplicity Pattern	1.30	C
Warner Communications	1.35	C

134

TABLE XIX

Volatility and Safety Ratings of PBW Exchange Options

Common Stock	Beta Coefficient	Quality
Abbot Laboratories	1.05	B
Allied Chemical	1.10	C
Boise Cascade	1.35	C
Continental Oil	1.10	B
Engelhard Minerals	1.15	C
Firestone Tire	1.00	C
Howard Johnson	1.50	C
Louisiana Land	1.10	C
Virginia Electric	.90	B
Woolworth	1.05	C

CHAPTER 9

Hedging and Spreading

Options may be used in hedging transactions to protect or insure against possible losses on securities in many ways. A call can be bought to reduce risk on a short sale or a put purchased to limit the potential loss on a long position in the underlying stock. Similarly, a call can be written to reduce the potential loss on a stock or an option.

Using options to hedge options is commonly called "spreading." This merely means buying an option and simultaneously selling short another option on the same stock. The options are exercisable at different prices or at different expiration dates. One may be long at one exercise price and short at another, or long a near month and short a far month, or the other way around.

Among the alternative arrangements are horizontal, vertical, sandwich, diagonal and variable spread positions. In a calendar or horizontal position, a far month may be held side by side with a near month sold short, or vice versa. In a vertical or perpendicular position, you may be long on one exercise price and short at another, so that one is above and one is below the other. In a butterfly spread or sandwich, two short positions at the middle exercise price may be inserted between one long at the highest exercise price and one long position at the lowest exercise price. In a diagonal position, you may be long a far month at one exercise price and short a near month at another exercise price, or the other way around. A variable spread position involves writing two or more call contracts on each round lot of the underlying stock held.

While hedging may mean risk reduction, spreading does not necessarily reduce risk. Spreading is tantamount to hedging only if the long end of a spread limits the potential loss of the short end. If the short position has a later expiration date than the long position, then the short end is not covered and such situation is a "naked" spread, instead of a real hedge.

The simultaneous buying and selling of options to achieve maximum exposure to possible profit with minimum risk could be a misconception or even a delusion. Unless one buys cheap calls and sells overpriced options, a typical spread actually exposes an investor to risk while offering profits only over a limited price range. Spreading appears enticing, but the results in the long run could clearly prove to be disappointing.

HORIZONTAL SPREAD

In a calendar or horizontal spread position, a call with a far expiration date must be bought and a call with a near expiration date sold short on the same stock at the same striking price, for the long end of the spread to limit the potential loss of the short end. For example, suppose a spread position is taken by buying a six-month XYZ April 40 call at 6 and simultaneously selling a three-month XYZ Jan 40 call at 4. In this case, the risk is limited to

138

the $200 difference between the premiums plus transaction costs. If the price of the underlying stock rises above the striking price so that the short end of the spread is exercised, you could simply exercise your long call and deliver the shares. However, if the price of the stock declines and the short end of the spread lapses, the premium received on the worthless option reduces the net cost of the long option to only $200 (before commissions). Thus, the option holder may retain a cheap call with a high profit potential for the next three months or possibly realize a profit by closing out the transaction if the underlying stock remains within a narrow price range.

It must be noted, however, that the typical horizontal spread can produce profits only if the price of the stock remains within a narrow price range during the period of the spread position. A broad movement in the price of the underlying stock will usually produce losses.

PERPENDICULAR POSITION

In a vertical or perpendicular position, the spread is initiated by buying a cheap call trading close to its intrinsic value and simultaneously selling short another call on the same stock with the same expiration date but at a different striking price. For example, suppose a call at 20 is purchased for a $200 premium and a call at 25 sold short for a $100 premium. In this case, the risk is limited to the $100 difference between the two premiums (plus transaction costs) should both options expire worthless. At the other extreme, if the price of the underlying stock rises above 25 so that the call at 25 would be exercised, you could simply exercise your call at 20 and deliver the shares for 25. Your profit would thus amount to $400 less transaction costs.

Since the potential profit on this perpendicular spread tends to become larger as the price of the underlying stock advances until it exceeds the higher of the two exercise prices, this spread seems specially attractive when you are "bullish" on the underlying stock.

A vertical spread can also work in reverse during a declining market. For example, suppose the stock sells above 25 and the spread between the two option prices is 4 points. Then you buy a cheap call at 25 and simultaneously sell short a call at 20. Since now you are purchasing the lower-priced call and selling the higher-priced option, you receive the $400 difference less commissions. This net difference represents the maximum possible profit, should the stock price fall below 20 so that both options expire worthless. At the other extreme, should the price of the stock rise, the risk is limited to the 5 point spread in the exercise prices minus the 4 points difference received, a maximum risk of $100 plus commissions. This relatively small risk, in contrast with the much larger potential profit, makes this reverse spread seem attractive.

SANDWICH

The "butterfly" or sandwich spread requires three levels of exercise prices at the same expiration date with the same number of points between each price level (such as 50, 60 and 70). You may buy one call at the highest exercise price and one at the lowest exercise price and simultaneously sell two at the middle exercise price for equal money. The possible loss will be limited to the amount of commissions, if the price of the underlying stock either declines below the lowest exercise price or rises above the highest exercise price. This spread will be profitable if the price of the stock remains near the middle exercise price.

For example, suppose you purchase one XRX July 50 at 10 and one XRX July 70 at 4 and simultaneously sell two XRX July 60 at 7. Should the price of the stock fall under 50 or rise over 70, the loss would be limited to the amount of the commissions. The maximum possible profit of $1,000 (before transaction costs) would be realized at a price of 60 upon expiration.

140

A "butterfly" or sandwich spread seems to offer moderate profit potential at limited risk, but the commission costs can prove to be very substantial. After paying from four to eight commissions on a single sandwich spread, the net profit may fail to provide a satisfactory return on investment. Moreover, nearly half of the sandwich spreads should show no net profit, after deducting the substantial transaction expenses and capital costs. A person seduced into sandwich spreads is like a butterfly flitting aimlessly from one thing to another.

DIAGONAL SPREAD

In a diagonal spread position, both the striking prices and the expiration dates on both options are different. One option is hedged against the other by buying a call with a far expiration date and simultaneouly selling short another call with a near expiration date on the same stock. For instance, suppose a six-month call at 80 is purchased for $600 and a three-month call at 90 on the same stock sold short for $200. In this case, the risk is limited to the $400 difference between the premiums plus transaction costs should both options expire worthless, since the call at 90 cannot ever be worth more than the call at 80. At the other extreme, should the price of the underlying stock rise above 90 so that the call at that striking price would be exercised, you could exercise your option

Potential profit	$600
less commissions	—200
Net profit potential	$400
Net risk	400
plus commissions	50
Gross risk	$450

141

at 80 and deliver the shares for 90 in order to realize a profit of $600 before transaction costs.

Since the risk-reward ratio in this case is significantly less than one, this example illustrates an unattractive spread. This kind of spread position in the long run could result in large losses and a negative return on invested capital, because of relatively large commission costs in spreading.

VARIABLE SPREAD

A variable spread position involves writing two or more call contracts on each round lot of the underlying stock held. This spread arrangement predicates movements in the value of an option are generally less than dollar-for-dollar in relation to price movements in the underlying stock (except for deep "in the money" options). Therefore, if the price of an option changes less than the price of the stock, it may be appropriate to write a multiple number of options against each round lot of covering stock, in orded to establish a more completely hedged position.

For instance, in the case of an exercise price of an option approximating the market price of the underlying stock, a one-half point change in the price of the option is likely for each point change in the stock, so that two options might be written for each round lot of stock held. In the case of an exercise price far above the stock price, this relationship could be three or four to one. The change in option value corresponding to a point change in the price of the underlying stock declines as the option moves further "out of the money," so that more and more calls might be written as the market price of the stock falls farther below the striking price of the option.

To illustrate a variable spread, suppose 100 shares of stock were purchased at 40 and a call written at that price for a 5 point premium, thereby providing downside protection against loss on the investment in the stock down to a price of 35. Instead of writing only one call, the sale of two options for two 5 point premiums provides a hedge against loss all the way down to a price of 30. If the price of the stock rises, any loss on the calls would offset the 10 point premiums received only when the price passes 50. In effect, this variable spread position proves profitable should the stock stay within the 30 to 50 band.

If the stock approaches the upper limit of this safety band, a call could be bought back to prevent a loss. On the other hand, if the stock price falls to the lower limit of this safety band, both options could be bought back at a nominal price. Then two new calls might be written for additional premiums, thereby providing further downside protection against loss on the stock.

A variable spread position can act as a defensive cushion in a declining market. The more calls sold per round lot of stock provide more protection against a slide, but less protection against a rise in the price of the underlying stock.

"SWEETHEART" SPREAD

An enticing type of variable spread is the so-called "sweetheart" spread position. Such a spread may enable one to score a profit within predetermined limits, regardless of the direction of the market movement of the price of the underlying stock—upward or downward.

One may buy one call and simultaneously sell short two calls on the same stock at a higher exercise price, or buy two and sell three, or engage in other possible combinations. In this illustration, sup-pose that when Polaroid common stock sold at 20, you bought an Oct 15 call for $700 and sold two Oct 20 calls for $450 each.

The following table shows the profit on the expiration date, assuming various possible prices of the underlying stock (ignoring commission costs). Shown on the long side is the gain or loss that would be realized by exercising the call, less the $700 option price paid for the call. Shown on the short side is the $900 premium received from the sale of the two options, less the loss on the exercise of these calls. The profit column shows the sum total of the long and short positions.

POLAROID "SWEETHEART" SPREAD

Price of Stock	Net Profit	Long @ 15	Short @ 20
14	$+200	$—700	$+900
15	+200	—700	+900
16	+300	—600	+900
17	+400	—500	+900
18	+500	—400	+900
19	+600	—300	+900
20	+700	—200	+900
21	+600	—100	+700
22	+500	—	+500
23	+400	+100	+300
24	+300	+200	+100
25	+200	+300	—100
26	+100	+400	—300

Since one call is purchased for $700 and two calls are sold for a total of $900, you get a net credit of $200 immediately. Should the stock sell at 15 or below on the expiration date, you will make a minimum profit of $200. As the stock sells above 15, the potential profit is progressively greater until it reaches a maximum of $700 at a price of 20. If the stock sells above 20, the profit diminishes. When the stock sells above 27, your "sweetheart" spread position will show a loss. This loss would become progressively larger as the price advances above 27.

144

The "sweetheart" spread position enhances both the potential profit and the risk involved in spreading, because the long end of such spread does not fully cover the short end. At some point, as the price of the underlying stock rises, a "sweetheart" spread be-comes in effect an uncovered or "naked" spread position exposed to substantial upside risk.

COVERT HEDGING

Surely safer than a "naked sweetheart" spread position is the more legitimate or conventional means of hedging by covered call writing. Initially, a long position in the stock is hedged by the sale of a call on the same stock. Then the subsequent strategy varies with the three different possible outcomes. To illustrate, suppose that in January 100 shares of Polaroid stock were purchased at $20 and a July call at 25 sold for $400. Here are the three dif-ferent possible outcomes:

OUTCOME A

If the price of the stock declines, the option writer has downside price protection equal to the amount of the premium received on the sale of the call. Should the price of the stock fall so sharply that exercise of the call is highly unlikely, the option could be repur-chased profitably at a mere fraction of the premium received to offset up to a 4 point loss on the stock. Then another call could be sold, thereby receiving an additional premium providing further downside price protection.

OUTCOME B

If the price of the stock remains unchanged or advances but fails to surpass the striking price of 25, the call is likely to expire unex-ercised. The $400 premium from the lapsed option pocketed as or-dinary income would represent a 25% return on the $1,600 net in-vestment ($2,000 minus $400) in six months, or 50% annualized. Then another covered call could be written against the same stock, thereby receiving an additional premium providing further down-side price protection.

If the price of the stock rises sharply to over 25, the call would be exercised and the writer would realize a $900 capital gain on the stock. This would represent a 56% return in six months, or 112% annualized.

"SWEETHEART" STRADDLE

Safer as well as more profitable than the "sweetheart" spread position is the "sweetheart" straddle. This kind of spread position also enables one to make a profit within predetermined bounds whether the price of the underlying stock moves up or down.

In this example, suppose that when Polaroid stock sold at 20, you wrote at that price nine-month options including a "naked" call for $450 and a put for $450. Hence, your account would show a total credit of $900 immediately.

The following table shows the profit on the expiration date, assuming various possible prices of the underlying stock (ignoring commission costs). Shown in the put column is the $450 premium received from the sale of a put, less the loss on any exercise of the put at such price. Shown in the call column is the $450 premium received from the sale of the call, less the loss on any exercise of the call at such price.

In this illustration, the maximum profit of $900 will be realized if the stock sells at 20 on the expiration date. As the price of the stock moves from this level in either direction, the potential profit becomes progressively smaller. Should the price rise to 29 or fall to 11, you will break even. If the stock departs from this price range, a loss would be incurred.

It is noteworthy that this "sweetheart" straddle provides a very wide safety band from as low as 11 to all the way up to 29. This safety band amounting to some 18 points almost equals the striking price of 20. In fact, the safety band provided by a "sweetheart" straddle is generally greater than that provided by a "sweetheart" spread position.

146

Polaroid "Sweetheart" Straddle

Price of Stock	Total Profit	Put	Call
12	$+100	$—350	$+450
13	+200	—250	+450
14	+300	—150	+450
15	+400	— 50	+450
16	+500	+ 50	+450
17	+600	+150	+450
18	+700	+250	+450
19	+800	+350	+450
20	+900	+450	+450
21	+800	+450	+350
22	+700	+450	+250
23	+600	+450	+150
24	+500	+450	+ 50
25	+400	+450	— 50
26	+300	+450	—150
27	+200	+450	—250
28	+100	+450	—350

VARIABLE STRADDLE

A variable straddle involves writing two or more call contracts against each put option sold. Whenever the price of a stock on which a put has been written declines by as much as 10% below the exercise price of the option, a call could be sold short. Should the market price of the underlying stock fall farther to 20% below the exercise price of the put, a second call could be sold short.

147

If the price of the stock falls by as much as 30% below the exercise price of the put, then a third call could be sold short. More and more calls might be written as the market price of the stock falls farther below the striking price of the put.

To illustrate this variable straddle, suppose a put were written at 50 for a 5 point premium, thereby providing downside protection against loss on the option in the stock down to a price of 45. If the market price of the underlying stock falls to 45, a call could be sold short for an additional premium providing further downside protection against loss on the put, down to around 40.

Should the price of the stock continue to slide, then more and more calls could be sold short for additional premiums providing further downside protection. In this way, a variable straddle position can act as a defensive cushion in a declining market. The more calls sold per put provide protection against a slide, but less protection against a rise in the price of the underlying stock.

On the other hand, should the price of the underlying stock rise substantially after a call has been sold short, another put might be written to provide upside protection against loss on the call. Whenever the price of the stock on which a call has been written increases by as much as 10% above the exercise price of the call, a new put could be sold for an additional premium providing protection against loss on the call. If the price of the underlying stock then returns to the exercise price of the call, a new call could be sold short at a higher exercise price providing an additional premium.

CHAPTER 10

Margin Requirements

The sale of an option does not generally take place in a cash account, because margin or assurance money or its equivalent is necessary to ensure that the option writer will fulfill his obligation to the option holder in the event of the exercise of the option. The execution of an option writing transaction in a cash account is precluded unless the account contains the underlying security, or an option guarantee letter or an escrow receipt of a bank custodian or trust company. In the case of a call, an option guarantee letter or an escrow receipt ensures that the custodian will deliver against payment the underlying security should the option be exercised. In the case of a put, an option guarantee ensures that the bank will make payment upon delivery of the security to the custodian should the opton be exercised.

No margin is required on an option in a covered writing position. Where a call is written against an existing "long" position

149

or a put written against an existing "short" position, no margin need be required on the call or put, provided such "long" or "short" position is adequately margined.

All other option writing transactions take place in a margin account. The amount of credit (if any) which may be initially extended by a broker or dealer at a time a customer enters into any securities transaction is governed by Regulation T of the Federal Reserve Board. In addition, the various securities exchanges impose their own minimum margin requirements that must be constantly maintained. Many brokers, moreover, impose more stringent requirements on their customers. Margin requirements are not uniform and are subject to change from time to time. Therefore, an investor should determine the margin obligations that will be imposed upon him by his broker, before engaging in any transaction in a margin account.

OPTION PURCHASES

Under Regulation T of the Federal Reserve Board or the rules of the New York Stock Exchange, neither puts nor calls have any value for loan purposes, so that option buyers must pay cash in full. Any stock acquired through the exercise of an option must be margined in accordance with Regulation T. However, if a call is exercised and the acquired shares are sold the same day, the deposit required is only 25% margin or $2,000, whichever is greater (except that cash need not be deposited in excess of the cost of any security bought).

NAKED UNLISTED OPTIONS

Under the new rules of the New York Stock Exchange promulgated in 1975, the minimum amount of margin that endorsing firms must require from writers of "naked" conventional options traded in over-the-counter market is 50% of the market value of the underlying security. Where both a put and a call contract for the same number of shares of the same underlying security are endorsed (as in the case of a straddle or spread option), the margin required is the margin on the put or call, whichever is greater.

The New York Stock Exchange requires that an option writer maintain this 50% margin throughout the life of the option. Hence, in case of a loss, the writer must furnish 100% of the price differential between the initial and the current market price of the stock, plus 50% of this differential for call options or minus 50% of the differential for put options. For example, a writer sells a conventional call on a stock at 50 and deposits the required 50% margin amounting to $2,500. Suppose the stock then rises to 60, so that the writer then has only a $1,500 equity on securities valued at $6,000. Therefore, he must deposit an additional $1,500 to bring his equity up to 50% of the current market value of the underlying stock. In effect, the writer of an uncovered or "naked" call is in the same position as a speculator selling stock short.

On the other hand, suppose a writer sells a put on a stock at 50 and deposits the required 50% margin amounting to $2,500. Should the price of the stock subsequently fall to 40, the writer then has only a $1,500 equity in a potential purchase of securities valued at $4,000. Therefore, an additional $500 must be deposited to bring his equity up to the required 50% of the current market value of the underlying stock.

If a broker allows an option writer to deposit minimum margin, the necessary amount of the out-of-pocket deposit on a call option is actually less than 50% of the market value of the stock, inasmuch as the premium received by the writer may be applied to the margin requirement. For example, suppose an option writer receives a $500 premium for a call on a stock at 40. Since the margin requirement is $2,000 (50% of $4,000) less the $500 premium, he must deposit only $1,500. Similarly, if a writer receives a $400 premium for a put on a stock at 40, he must deposit only $1,600, because the minimum margin requirement is $2,000 (50% of $4,000) less the $400 premium.

151

"NAKED" LISTED OPTIONS

The New York Stock Exchange has promulgated for its members margin rules on Exchange Traded Options, such as Chicago Board Options or options listed on the American Stock Exchange. The margin requirement for an uncovered "short" listed call option is 30% of the market value of the underlying security. This 30% requirement must be increased by the amount the market value of the underlying security exceeds the exercise price of the call option (in the money) or decreased by the amount the market value of the underlying security is below the exercise price of the call option (out of the money).

For example, suppose a "naked" XRX July 50 call is sold for $10 when the market price of XRX stock is $50. The margin computation would be:

30% of the underlying security ($5,000 x .3)	$1,500
Proceeds of the option sale	—1,000
Net margin requirement	$ 500

If the price of the underlying stock moves up to $60, the margin computation would be:

30% of the underlying security ($6,000 x .3)	$1,800
In the money ($6,000 —$5,000)	1,000
Maintenance margin requirement	$2,800

If the price of the underlying stock subsequently moves down to $40, the margin computation would be:

30% of the underlying security ($4,000 x .3)	$1,200
Out of the money ($4,000 —$5,000)	—1,000
Maintenance margin requirement	$ 200*

---

* Since a $250 minimum must be maintained for each "naked" option contract, the maintenance margin requirement would be $250 and not $200.

The New York Stock Exchange has formally established a $250 minimum margin requirement for each "short" uncovered option in a customer's account, regardless of whether it is a conventional option traded in the over-the-counter market or a listed option traded on an organized exchange (such as a Chicago Board Option).

SPREADS

Also introduced were new margin requirements with regard to hedging of listed call options. Where a call is carried "long" and the account is also "short" a call expiring on or before the "long" call and written on the same number of shares of the same security, the margin required on the "short" call is the lower of the 30% requirement for a "naked" option or the amount, if any, by which the exercise price of the "long" call exceeds the exercise price of the "short" call. To qualify a "spread" for purposes of this rule, the "long" option may not expire before the "short" option expires. If the "long" option expires prior to the "short" option, the "short" option must be margined as a "naked" or an uncovered short position.

For example, suppose ATT April 40 is bought for 5 and ATT Jan 40 simultaneously sold short for 3 with the market price of ATT common stock at 40. This spread qualifies for the special spread margin treatment, because the long option expires after the short option. The margin requirement would be the lesser of:

30% of the underlying security ($4,000 x .3) $1,200

or

Difference beteen exercise price (40 — 40)   0

In this spread, no margin is required on the short position. The $300 proceeds of the sale of the short position may be applied toward the $500 purchase price of the long position. This means that only an additional $200 is needed to satisfy the requirement that the payment on a long option must be in full.

153

For example, assume that IBM Jan 180 is purchased for 20 and IBM Jan 160 simultaneously sold short for 35 with the price of IBM stock at 190. Since the long option expires on the same date as the short option, this spread also qualifies for the special spread margin treatment. The margin requirement would be the lesser of:

30% of the underlying security ($19,000 x .3) $5,700

In the money (190 — 160) 3,000

Requirement $8,700

or

Difference between exercise prices (180 — 160) $2,000

In this case, the margin requirement on the short position is $2,000. The $3,500 proceeds of the option sold minus the $2,000 payment for the option purchased contribute $1,500 toward satisfying this $2,000 requirement. This means that an additional $500 is needed to satisfy the $2,000 requirement.

If the price of the underlying stock subsequently drops to 120, the margin requirement would be the lesser of:

30% of the underlying security (1,200 x .3) $3,600

Out of the money (120 — 160) ....—4,000

Requirement 0

or

Difference between exercise prices (180 — 160) $2,000

Consequently, the maintenance margin requirement on this spread position is reduced to zero.

In another case, suppose ATT Jan 40 is purchased for 3 and ATT April 40 simultaneously sold short for 5 with the market price of ATT common stock at 40. This spread position does not qualify for the special margin treatment, because the "long" option expires prior to the "short" option. Consequently, the short position must be treated as a "naked" call option for margin purposes.

CONVERTIBLE COVER

In those cases where a "short" call option is hedged by a "long" position in a security exchangeable or convertible into the same security under option (such as a warrant or a convertible bond), the required margin must be increased by the amount, if any, by which the conversion price of the "long" security exceeds the exercise price of the "short" call. The margin requirement in effect is the lower of either the requirement for a "naked" short listed option or the amount by which any amount of money payable upon such exchange or conversion exceeds the exercise price of the "short" option.

For example, suppose you own 100 ATT warrants convertible into 100 shares of ATT common stock at 52 with a market price of $1 per warrant and sell an ATT Jan 40 option at 3 with the market price of ATT common stock at 40. The margin requirement on the short option position would be the lesser of:

30% of the underlying security ($4,000 x .3) $1,200

or

Amount payable upon warrant conversion $5,200

Exercise price of option ....—4,000

Margin required $1,200

After allowing for the $300 proceeds from the option sold, an additional deposit of $900 is necessary to satisfy the margin requirement on the short option position in this hedge.

If the price of the underlying stock subsequently falls to 35, the margin requirement would be the lesser of:

155

30% of the underlying security ($3,500 x .3) $1,050

Out of the money (40 — 35) .... —500
_____

Margin required .... $ 550

or

Amount payable upon Warrant conversion $5,200

Exercise price of option ....—4,000
_____

$1,200

Consequently, the maintenance margin requirement on the short option position in this hedge is reduced to $550.

ESCROW RECEIPT

Transactions in options may be effected in a special cash account if the underlying securities are held in the account. Also sufficient for this purpose is an option guarantee letter or an escrow receipt of a bank custodian guaranteeing that the underlying security is held in the customer's account and will be delivered in the event of the exercise of the option.

The Options Clearing Corporation facilitates the use of escrow receipts by providing a standard form for listed options sold on an organized securities exchange, such as a Chicago Board Option or an option traded on the American Stock Exchange. The New York Stock Exchange permits any customer of a member firm to deposit fully paid stock (in the case of a call) or cash (in the case of a put), against which options will be endorsed, in a bank or trust company escrow account, provided the custodian bank or trust company is prepared to issue an option guarantee letter in a form acceptable to the New York Stock Exchange or to the option endorsing member firm. Besides allowing the use of the standard Escrow Receipt form for listed options issued by the Options Clearing Corporation, the New York Stock Exchange has prepared separate standard forms for "Put" or "Call" Option Guarantee Letters.

156

Where statutory requirements preclude financial institutions from leaving securities or other assets with a broker or a dealer, this problem in writing options is thus overcome by the use of either an Escrow Receipt for listed options or an Option Guarantee Letter for unlisted options.

As a matter of fact, any covered option writer may arrange for an Escrow Receipt or an Option Guarantee Letter. In such an arrangement, transactions in options may be effected in a special cash account and no margin deposit is required in option writing.

If an option writer has adequate capital in escrow to ensure his obligations, it is not necessary to tie capital to any particular option written. He could deposit cash or its equivalent or other securities with the bank custodian to assure his obligations to option holders in the event of the exercise of options. Hence, it is not absolutely necessary for a writer to cover every option with the particular shares of the underlying stock.

COLLATERAL

Rather than employing cash, an option writer may satisfy margin requirements with his broker by depositing as collateral other marginable securities with loan value at least equal to the margin required. In this computation, the loan value of a security is equal to 100% minus the amount of the margin requirement on that security. For example, the initial margin requirement on U.S. Government bonds is 10%, so that their loan value is 90% (100% minus 10%).

TABLE XX
Collateral Loan Values
(as of August 1, 1975)

Type of Security	Initial	Maintenance
Listed stock	50%	75%
Convertible bonds	50	75
Non-convertible bonds	70	75
Municipals	85	90
U.S. Governments	90	95

157

THE OPTIONS CLEARING CORPORATION   ER-1   010776

Escrow Receipt

date _____

To: (Clearing Member name)
and The Options Clearing Corporation

The undersigned hereby represents and warrants that (a) it is a bank or trust company organized under the laws of the United States or a state thereof and supervised and examined by state or federal authority having supervision over banks or trust companies; (b) the equity attributable to all outstanding shares of capital stock issued by the undersigned is not less than $20,000,000; and (c) the total market value of all shares of stock held by it pursuant to all outstanding escrow receipts (including this Escrow Receipt) substantially similar hereto and all outstanding guarantee letters relating to "calls", plus the total dollar amount held by it on deposit pursuant to all outstanding guarantee letters relating to "puts", does not exceed a dollar amount equal to 10% of the equity attributable to all outstanding shares of capital stock issued by the undersigned.

The undersigned certifies that it holds _____ shares of

_____
(type of security—e.g., Common Stock)

of _____
     (name of issuer)

(the "deposited securities") as custodian for _____
                                                    (name of customer)

that the deposited securities are in good deliverable form (or the undersigned has the unrestricted power to put the deposited securities into good deliverable form) in accordance with the requirements of the New York Stock Exchange (or such other exchange as may be the primary market for such securities), and that such customer has specifically authorized the undersigned to file this Escrow Receipt with you and to hold the deposited securities as an escrow deposit pursuant to the Rules of The Options Clearing Corporation (the "Corporation") in respect of such customer's position ("short position") as a writer of the following Exchange Traded Option contract(s) to purchase the deposited securities:

Number of Contracts	Option Series	
	Expiration Month and Year	Exercise Price

158

The undersigned further certifies and agrees that it will hold the deposited securities in accordance with the terms of this Escrow Receipt and will deliver all or any part of the deposited securities at the order of the Corporation or the above-named Clearing Member ("Clearing Member") in the event the Corporation or such Clearing Member notifies the undersigned that an exercise notice filed with the Corporation in respect of one or more such option contracts has been assigned to the aforesaid short position, against payment of the exercise price of such option contract(s) less all applicable commissions and other charges. The undersigned further agrees that (a) the deposited securities shall remain in the custody of the undersigned until this Escrow Receipt is returned to the undersigned by the endorsement set forth below or this Escrow Receipt expires as hereinafter provided, (b) the Corporation shall have the right to hold this Escrow Receipt until it is satisfied, upon the filing by the aforesaid Clearing Member of a withdrawal request pursuant to the Rules of the Corporation, that all margin required in respect of the aforesaid short positions has been deposited with the Corporation, if an exercise notice has been assigned to such short position, until either the requisite deposited securities shall have been delivered pursuant to such assignment, and (c) the Corporation shall have the right to assign an exercise notice in respect of the aforesaid short position so long as it holds this Escrow Receipt.

In the event there is a distribution of any securities or other property ("distributed property") in respect of the deposited securities as a result of any dividend, stock dividend, stock distribution, stock split, rights offering, distribution, reorganization, recapitalization or reclassification, or other similar event, which results in an adjustment in any of the above-listed option contracts pursuant to Section II of Article VI of the Corporation's By-Laws, the term "deposited securities" as used herein shall be deemed to include the distributed property from and after the date of such distribution, and the term "short position" as used herein shall be deemed to include the above-listed option contracts as so adjusted from and after the ex-date for such distribution. In the event the Corporation shall assign an exercise notice in respect of the short position between the ex-date for such distribution and the time of such distribution, the undersigned agrees to deliver the distributed property pursuant to the instructions of the Corporation not later than 5 business days following the receipt of such distribution.

This Escrow Receipt shall expire and be of no further effect on the earlier of (a) the date the Corporation returns it (as evidenced by its endorsement of release below) or (b) the close of business on the Corporation's second full business day in the calendar month immediately following the expiration month set forth above; provided, however, that if an exercise notice has been assigned to such short position this Escrow Receipt shall not expire until and unless the Corporation has endorsed its release below.

As between the undersigned and the Corporation, this Escrow Receipt represents an obligation of the undersigned generally, rather than an obligation of the undersigned in any particular capacity, or as a fiduciary with respect to any particular account (although, as between the undersigned and the customer, the fiduciary obligations of the undersigned shall not be impaired hereby).

_____
(custodian)

by: _____

Endorsement of release
The Corporation hereby returns and releases all of its rights and the rights of the Clearing Member with respect to this Escrow Receipt.
The Options Clearing Corporation

by _____

date _____

159

_____ (Date) _____

TO: (New York Stock Exchange Member Firm)

The undersigned (the Bank) having an office located at _____
_____, hereby represents and warrants that:

.. (i) it is a bank or trust company, doing business in corporate form, organized under the laws of the United States or any State thereof and is supervised and examined by State or Federal authority having supervision over banks or trust companies; and

(ii) the total dollar amount held by it on deposit pursuant to all outstanding guarantee letters relating to "puts" (including this letter) substantially similar to this letter, plus the total market value of all shares of stock held by it pursuant to all guarantee letters relating to "calls" (including all outstanding Escrow Receipts addressed to any options exchange), does not exceed a dollar amount equal to 10% of the equity attributable to all outstanding shares of capital stock issued by the Bank; and

'(iii) the Bank has received specific authorization from the Customer to issue this guarantee letter and to hold the amount described herein pursuant to the provisions hereof.

The Bank represents and warrants that it has on deposit for the account of _____ (the Customer) $_____ (the Purchase Price) and in consideration of your endorsing a "put" on ____ shares of _____ stock executed by the Customer, the Bank hereby undertakes and agrees that until the Expiration Date hereinafter defined it will continue to hold the Purchase Price and that the Purchase Price will be paid to you at any time on or before the Expiration Date, plus commissions and other applicable charges against delivery by you to the Bank for the account of the Customer of _____ shares of _____ stock endorsed in blank in form to constitute good delivery under the rules of the New York Stock Exchange, Inc.

In the event of any cash or stock dividend, stock distribution, stock split, rights offering, distribution, reorganization, recapitalization or reclassification, or other similar event, the Purchase Price to be paid to you against delivery as hereinabove provided, or the shares of stock to be delivered by you against payment as hereinabove provided, shall be adjusted, increased or decreased in accordance with the terms of the "put".

Delivery and payment as aforesaid shall be made at the office of the Bank shown above.

This guarantee letter represents an obligation of the Bank generally, rather than an obligation of the Bank in any particular capacity, or as a fiduciary with respect to any particular account.

As used herein the term "Expiration Date" shall mean the close of business on the ____ day of _____, 197_ (the second full business day immediately following the expiration date of the "put"), except that if, on or prior to the expiration date of the "put", the Bank is notified by you that the "put" has been exercised, the Expiration Date shall not occur until the Bank has completed payment of the total amount due to you hereunder against delivery of shares in accordance with the provisions hereof. This guarantee letter shall expire and be of no further effect from and after the Expiration Date.

(BANK)

By_____
Authorized Signature

OPTION GUARANTEE LETTER
"CALL"

_____ (Date) _____

TO: (New York Stock Exchange Member Firm)

      The undersigned (the Bank) having an office located at _____
_____, hereby represents and warrants that:

      (i) it is a bank or trust company, doing business in corporate
form, organized under the laws of the United States or any State
thereof and is supervised and examined by State or Federal authority
having supervision over banks or trust companies; and

      (ii) the total market value of all shares of stock held by it
pursuant to all outstanding guarantee letters relating to "calls" (including this letter) substantially similar to this letter - (including
all outstanding Escrow Receipts addressed to any options exchange),
plus the total dollar amount held by it on deposit pursuant to all
outstanding guarantee letters relating to "puts", does not exceed a
dollar amount equal to 10% of the equity attributable to all outstanding shares of capital stock issued by the Bank; and

      (iii) the Bank has received specific authorization from the Cus-
tomer to issue this guarantee letter and to hold the securities described herein pursuant to the provisions hereof.

      The Bank represents and warrants that it holds for the account of
_____ (the Customer), _____ shares of _____
stock (the Deposited Securities), and in consideration of your endorsing a
"call" on the Deposited Securities executed by the Customer, the Bank hereby
undertakes and agrees that until the Expiration Date hereinafter defined it
will continue to hold the Deposited Securities and that the Deposited Securities
will be delivered to you at any time on or before the Expiration Date endorsed
in blank in form to constitute a good delivery under the Rules of the New York
Stock Exchange, Inc. against payment by you to the Bank for the account of the
Customer of $_____, minus all applicable commissions and other charges.

      In the event of any cash or stock dividend, stock distribution, stock
split, rights offering, distribution, reorganization, recapitalization or reclassification, or other similar event, the Deposited Securities to be delivered
to you against payment as hereinabove provided, or the amount to be paid by you
against delivery as hereinabove provided, or both, shall be adjusted, increased
or decreased in accordance with the terms of the "call".

      The Bank agrees that all necessary stock transfer stamps shall be
affixed to the "call".

      Delivery and payment as aforesaid shall be made at the office of the Bank
shown above.

      This guarantee letter represents an obligation of the Bank generally,
rather than an obligation of the Bank in any particular capacity, or as a
fiduciary with respect to any particular account.

      As used herein the term "Expiration Date" shall mean the close of busi-
ness on the ____ day of _____, 197_ (the second full business day immediately
following the expiration date of the "call"), except that if, on or prior to the
expiration date of the "call", the Bank is notified by you that the "call" has
been exercised, the Expiration Date shall not occur until the Bank has completed
delivery of all the Deposited Securities against payment therefor in accordance
with the provisions hereof. This guarantee letter shall expire and be of no
further effect from and after the Expiration Date.

          (BANK)

          By_____
               Authorized Signature

CHAPTER 11

Summary and Conclusions

Ever since Jacob acquired a call on Rachel's hand and Joseph was conceived as the first dividend on an option some 4,000 years ago, put and call options have served many useful purposes.[1]

OPTION BUYING

An option may be bought to acquire leverage or unlimited opportunity for profit, while limiting the risk of loss in an investment or speculation. While the possible profit on the purchase of a call could be unlimited, the potential loss is limited to the cost of the option and that amount is known in advance.

Although options are commonly employed for speculation on a limited amount of capital, they can be used as a hedge or insurance on an existing position in a security. To protect a security position,

---

[1] The Bible—Genesis 29, 30 and 41.

a put may be purchased against a long position or a call may be bought against a short position in the stock. A bullish or optimistic speculator could buy a call or a bearish speculator could purchase a put. In fact, a put purchase is a superior substitute for selling stock short.

Unless the objective is hedging or insurance against loss on the underlying stock, put or call buying generally results in losses. However, if options are purchased at prices close to their intrinsic values or below their actuarial values, buying puts or calls could be profitable.

PUT PURCHASE

Though short selling is the traditional means of profiting from a fall in the price of a stock, a gain from any short sale is always considered a short-term capital gain for tax purposes, no matter how long a short position remained open. Short selling, moreover, is vulnerable to an extremely high degree of risk, because there is no limit to potential losses in such speculation.

Since a short sale is never eligible for long-term capital gains tax treatment, a put purchase is the only way a long-term capital gain could be realized on a short position in a declining market. A put is considered a capital asset, so that a profit on a put may qualify as a long-term capital gain taxable at a more favorable rate than a short sale. At a predetermined risk limited to the cost of the option, a put purchase gets greater percentage profit potential, in contrast with the unlimited loss potential of a short sale.

While the speculative use of a put as a superior substitute for a short sale of stock provides a leveraged short position, the employment of a put as insurance provides protection of a long position in the underlying stock as a hedge against a possible fall in the price of the stock. If the price falls precipitously, the put would be exercised to limit the loss to the cost of the option. But

164

if the price of the stock rises, the put should be allowed to lapse and the profit on the stock would be realized.

CALL BUYING

A call can provide protection against the possibility of unlimited loss on a short sale of stock, because this option gives its holder the privilege to purchase the underlying stock at a fixed striking price. If the market price of the stock soars, the call could be exercised and the stock delivered against the short position in order to limit the loss to the cost of the option. But if the price of the stock declines, the call would be allowed to lapse and the profit on the short sale should be realized.

Calls are commonly used to acquire leverage, while limiting the risk of loss to the cost of the option. A purchase of a call can get greater percentage profit potential than by buying the underlying stock outright or even on margin. This speculative use of a call anticipates a profit from an advance in the price of the stock. However, a call cannot become profitable until the underlying stock appreciates in value by more than the cost of the option.

OPTION WRITING

Whereas an option is purchased for the purpose of limiting the amount of loss in an investment or speculating for unlimited profit potential, writers of puts and calls are willing to acquire shares of stock at a lower price than the current market or to sell stock at a higher price than the current market. By selling a put, the premium received will reduce the cost of any shares acquired. By selling a call, the premium will increase the profit on any stock sold. If a put or a call expires unexercised, the option writer pockets the premium received.

In writing options, no single strategy is best for all possible purposes. The rate of return on investment clearly varies with the strategy as well as the tactics employing different types of option contracts. Certain option writing strategies, in fact, can attain substantially larger returns on investment than a buy and hold strategy.

PUT WRITING

A put writer is generally an investor willing to purchase shares of stock below their current market prices. By selling puts, an option writer receives premiums which will reduce the cost of any such shares acquired. Although the price of a stock might drop so precipitously as to saddle the writer with a sizable loss, the cost of the acquired shares is less than a direct purchase of the stock without writing the put. If the price of the underlying stock rises and the put lapses, the writer simply pockets the premium received.

Covered put writing, nevertheless, is not a common strategy. The so-called covered put writer, who sells short the underlying stock and sells a put against this short position, is not really hedged, but is completely and clearly exposed to the risk of unlimited losses should the price of the stock soar. For this reason, a conservative option writer ordinarily does not sell covered puts.

Unlike the unlimited risk exposure of the so-called covered put writer, the risk to a "naked" or uncovered put writer is surely limited to no more than the price of the underlying stock, less the amount of the premium received. The actual risk position of the "naked" put writer is virtually the equivalent of a covered call writer who hedges the sale of a call by buying or holding the underlying stock.

The sale of uncovered puts is generally profitable to the option writer. As a matter of fact, no known empirical study shows put writing to be unprofitable. The average annual rate of return on investment in put writing could come to some 10%. This average rate of return might actually be improved considerably if puts are sold at substantial premiums over their actuarial values.

166

COVERED CALL WRITING

A covered call writer is generally an investor willing to sell shares of stock above their current market price. By selling calls, an option writer receives premiums which will increase the proceeds of any such shares sold. The covered call writer is protected from the risk of unlimited loss involved in writing a call without owning the underlying stock and is thus unaffected by the extent to which the price of the stock rises. If the price of the stock declines and the option expires unexercised, the call writer retains the stock and pockets the premium received. While this writer loses from any downward price movement, no net loss is suffered unless the amount of the price decline exceeds the option premium. In any event, the covered call writer is in a better investment position than an investor in the same stock who has not received a premium.

Through the sale of covered calls, an option writer can in effect sell shares of stock above their current market price. The average annual rate of return on investment in covered calls could come to some 14%. This average rate of return might actually be surpassed significantly should calls be sold at substantial premiums above their actuarial values.

NAKED CALL WRITING

Unlike a covered call writer, a "naked" or uncovered call writer is not protected from the unlimited potential loss involved in writing a call option without owning the underlying stock. If the price of the stock rises, the option will be exercised and the "naked" writer would be required to buy the stock at the higher current market price to meet the call. Hence, an uncovered call writer is not an investor willing to sell shares of stock above their market price.

The uncovered call writer, however, is unaffected by the extent to which the price of the underlying stock falls and suffers no loss from any downward price movement. If the price of the stock drops, the "naked" call writer simply pockets the premium received and is ahead by that amount.

"Naked" or uncovered call writing really represents the equivalent of a short sale of the underlying security. Since the uncovered call writer is not at all protected against a rise in the price of the stock, his position is very vulnerable to the possibility of unlimited losses. The clear exposure to this risk makes an uncovered call writer surely a "naked" writer.

The sale of "naked" calls is neither safe nor necessarily profitable. The average annual rate of return on uncovered call writing may actually prove to be significantly smaller than the opportunity cost of available alternatives of investing directly in the underlying shares of common stock or even purchasing U.S. Government bonds. There is no preponderance of empirical evidence to clearly indicate that the writing of uncovered calls provides a satisfactory rate of return on investment. In any event, "naked" or uncovered call writing is unsafe at any rate.

STRADDLE WRITING

Option writers, who are willing to acquire stock at a price below the current market or to sell shares at a price above the current market, will write straddles. By combining the simultaneous sale of both puts and calls, straddle writing can produce greater premiums than selling individual puts or calls alone. If the price of the underlying stock declines, a put would be exercised and the straddle writer in effect would acquire shares below the current market prices. If the price of the stock remains unchanged, the put and call options would lapse and the straddle writer would simply pocket the dual premium.

By combining the simultaneous sale of both puts and calls, the average annual rate of return on covered straddle writing could come to about 24%. This average rate of return might actually be surpassed significantly should options be sold at substantial premiums over their actuarial values. This combination of holding a portfolio of common stocks and writing both puts and calls on these underlying securities tends to produce considerably larger returns on investment than a buy and hold strategy, though this straddle strategy entails little or no added risk.

As a variation of this straddle strategy, an option writer can in effect acquire shares of stock below their current market prices through the sale of puts. After such shares are purchased at reduced costs when the puts are exercised, the option writer could in effect sell such shares above their current market prices through the sale of covered calls.

In this way, an option writer may accumulate shares of stock when their prices are depressed and then dispose of such shares after a rise—a sound investment procedure!

RISKS AND SAFEGUARDS

Whereas the average annual rate of return on investment in options clearly varies with the type of option contract utilized as well as with the strategy selected, the actual return also depends upon the premiums paid for the actuarial value of the options. The spread between the option price and the actuarial value of the options may make the difference between profit or loss for the buyer or seller. Buyers who generally pay premiums for options in excess of their actuarial values must suffer losses in the long-run. Conversely, option writing can be profitable only if premiums consistently exceed the actuarial values of options sold. Therefore, whether option buyers or sellers gain or lose depends on option premiums.

While the sale of uncovered calls without owning the underlying securities may be the equivalent of indulging in investment streaking indelicately exposed to the naked risks of unlimited losses, the sale of covered options against a diversified portfolio

169

is no more speculative than owning the same stocks. A security portfolio must be diversified, to prevent undue risks arising out of extreme fluctuations in the market prices of individual stocks. To prevent undue risks associated with general market movements, option writing should be staggered over a period of time so that option expirations are not concentrated in any single month or two. A writer must have the necessary financial resources to honor obligations on all options written. In fact, an option, writer has no business dealing in securities that he could not or would not want to own.

CONCLUSIONS

1. A call may be bought to acquire leverage for greater profit potential in a rising market and to limit the amount of the potential loss to the cost of the option. Or a call could be purchased as a hedge or insurance against loss on a short position in the underlying stock.

2. A put purchase may be used as a superior substitute for a short sale of the underlying stock in a declining market or as a hedge or insurance against loss on a long position in the stock.

3. Writing an uncovered or "naked" call really represents the equivalent of a short position in the underlying stock. Like a short sale of the stock, a "naked" call provides profitable leverage in a declining market, but its return in a rising market is neither necessarily satisfactory nor safe at any rate of return.

4. Through the sale of puts, an option writer can in effect purchase shares of stock below their current market prices.

5. Through the sale of covered calls, an option writer can in effect sell shares of stock above their current market prices.

6. By combining the sale of both puts and calls at substantial premiums over their actuarial values, covered straddle writing can achieve an average annual rate of return on such investment amounting to possibly as much as 24% or even more.

7. As an adjunct to regular investment activities, the writing of both put and call options against a diversified portfolio of securities can produce substantially larger returns on investment than the ordinary buy and hold strategy, though this straddle strategy entails little or virtually no added risk.

By buying cheap puts or calls close to their intrinsic values, options can be used as attractive hedges or as insurance against short or long positions in the underlying stock. By selling puts and calls at substantial premiums above their actuarial values, covered option writing can raise the rate of return on investment in a diversified portfolio and also reduce the risk in holding such stocks.

Investors should seriously consider writing options against their portfolio, as an adjunct to their regular investment activities, in order to increase their investment yields substantially.

Appendix

COMPTROLLER OF CURRENCY RULING

THE ADMINISTRATOR OF NATIONAL BANKS

WASHINGTON, D.C. 20219

Trust Banking Circular No. 2

July 2, 1974

TO: Regional Administrators, Presidents of Banks with Fiduciary Powers
(Attention: Sr. Trust Officer) and Trust Examiners

SUBJECT: Dealing in Options on Securities in Trust Accounts

On November 8, 1973, we directed a letter to the presidents of all national banks with fiduciary powers, in which we set forth our position in reference to such banks dealing in options on securities in trust accounts. Essentially, that position was stated as being that since certain legal decisions implied that all option transactions are speculative as a matter of law, such transactions by national bank trust departments would be subject to criticism. Since our letter of November 8 we have received several memoranda from national banks and other interested parties dealing with our position. Most of the memoranda concur in our position except as to the writing of covered call options. The opinion was expressed that banks could safely engage in writing call options on securities held in inventory, subject to the prudent-man rule, under the present state of the law. Upon further consideration, we have decided to accept this position. Consequently, we shall not object to the writing of call options on securities held in trust department accounts where specific authority for such transactions is contained in the governing instrument of the particular account, and where the particular transaction is appropriate for the account. Also, we shall not object to transactions in other forms of options which are directly related to a covered call option which the bank has outstanding. For example, a bank could protect its position by purchasing a call on the same security as is presently subject to a call, to provide protection in a declining market. However, we feel that these other forms of options must be criticized when engaged in as an original investment.

We have also received several inquiries concerning our position regarding national banks acting as custodian or agent of securities for parties under option contracts and issuing escrow receipts and guarantee letters with respect to such contracts. The function of the bank under such an arrangement would be limited to holding the securities in escrow in order to assure that they would be available if the option is exercised. We feel that this participation by national banks in option transactions is readily distinguishable from the situation where the bank would be the writer or purchaser of an option contract. Consequently, we would not criticize banks for engaging in this activity.

James E. Smith
Comptroller of the Currency

175

INSURANCE DEPARTMENT OF THE STATE OF NEW YORK REGULATION NO. 72

(11 NYCCR 174)

SALE AND PURCHASE OF EXCHANGE TRADED CALL OPTIONS

I, BENJAMIN R. SCHENCK, Superintendent of Insurance of the State of New York, pursuant to the authority granted by Sections 10, 21 and Article V of the New York Insurance Law, do hereby promulgate the following Part 174 of Title 11 of the Official Compilation of Codes, Rules and Regulations (Regulation No. 72), to take effect after filing with the Secretary of State, on January 1, 1975, to read as follows:

Section 174.1 *Preamble*

This Department has ruled in the past that licensed insurance companies are prohibited from dealing in options on common stock.

The prohibition against selling options was based upon the following language of Section 78(2) of the Insurance Law:

> "The disposition of... [an insurer's] property shall be
> all times within the control of its board of directors. ..."

At the time these rulings were made, there was no organized and regulated market in which stock options could be traded. Nor were there readily ascertainable prices and terms for such transactions. Option contracts and trading practices were unregulated and unstandardized. In that context, the sale of an option could result in an insurer losing control of the underlying stock upon which the option was written, as the seller had little choice but to await either the exercise of an option by the holder or its expiration. With the advent of regulated option exchanges, this objection is no longer present. Options traded on a regulated exchange have standardized exercise prices and other terms, and the existence of such exchange enables an insurer to retain control of the stock upon which an option was written by providing a ready market for purchasing an option, the effect of which is to reduce or eliminate the outstanding written option.

The prohibition against purchasing options was based upon the following language in Section 80(3) of the Insurance Law:

> "No securities or other investments shall be eligible for
> purchase or acquisition under this section unless they are
> interest bearing or income paying..."

176

The advent of regulated options exchanges does not overcome the statutory objection to purchasing options, which practice remains prohibited except in the limited case of a closing purchase transaction in view of the actual effect thereof.

Insurers presently have the authority to buy and sell common stock. The sale of exchange-traded call options through an exchange, on stock which is already owned by an insurer, provides the insurer with a conservative money management tool by which it can minimize the risks inherent in the ownership of stock.

Section 174.2 *Definitions.*

For the purpose of this Regulation:

> (a) "call option" means an option contract under which the holder of the option has the right, in accordance with the terms of the option, to purchase the number of shares of the underlying stock covered by the option contract.

> (b) "exchange" means a national securities exchange registered under the Securities Exchange Act of 1934 which has been authorized to provide a market for option contracts pursuant to Rule 9b-1 under the Securities Exchange Act of 1934, as amended.

> (c) "exchange-traded" means traded on the floor of an exchange.

> (d) "escrow receipt" means an escrow receipt issued with respect to escrowed stock held on deposit by a bank or other custodian approved by a registered national securities exchange.

> (e) "escrowed stock" means stock owned by an insurance company with respect to which an escrow receipt has been issued.

> (f) "closing purchase transaction" means the purchase of an exchange-traded call option the effect of which is to reduce or eliminate the obligations of a call option writer with respect to an option contract or contracts.

Section 174.3 *Sale of Exchange-Traded Call Options*

An insurer may sell exchange-traded call options only through an exchange and only with respect to stock which it owns. Insurers may not sell any other options.

Any insurer selling an option: (a) shall enter into an escrow agreement which provides that its escrowed stock is kept segregated by the bank or other custodian from other securities owned by the company, and from securities owned by others, which are deposited with the same bank or other custodian, and (b) must obtain and retain in its possession a copy of an escrow receipt identifying with particularity the escrowed stock.

Section 174.4 *Purchase of Exchange-Traded Call Options*

An insurer may purchase an exchange-traded call option only through an exchange and only for the purpose of a closing purchase transaction. Insurers may not purchase any other options.

Section 174.5 *Accounting for Transactions in Exchange-Traded Call Options*

(a) The price received for selling a call option shall not be included in income at the time of receipt, but shall be carried in a deferred account until one of the following occurs: (1) the call option expires through the passage of time, (2) the company sells the underlying stock pursuant to an exercise of the call option, or (3) the company engages in a closing purchase transaction in respect thereto.

(b) If a call option expires through the passage of time, the price for the option shall be treated as investment income received at the time of such expiration.

(c) If the underlying stock is sold pursuant to the exercise of a call option, the price received for the option shall be treated as increasing the amount realized upon the sale of the stock and shall be included in determining capital gain or loss.

(d) If a call option is terminated through a closing purchase transaction, the difference between the price received from the sale of the call option and the price paid in the closing purchase transaction shall be treated, at the time of such closing purchase transaction, as an addition to or deduction from investment income, as the case may be.

Section 174.6 *Valuation*

Stock owned by an insurance company with respect to which a call option has been sold shall be valued, so long as the obligation under the option continues, at the lesser of the exercise price of the option or the current market price of the stock.

Section 174.7 *Prohibition against Speculating in Options*

The authority granted to insurers herein to engage in option transactions shall be used solely in a manner consistent with the insurer's obligation to exercise prudent judgment in the conservative management of its assets. Each option transaction shall reflect such prudent judgment and shall have a rationale related to such conservative management of assets rather than speculation. Nothing herein shall be construed to authorize an insurer to engage in option transactions to an extent or to a degree which would, under the relevant circumstances, be inordinate or speculative. The insurer shall establish and maintain records as to each transaction, demonstrating compliance with this section.

I, BENJAMIN R. SCHENK, Superintendent of Insurance of the State of New York, do hereby certify that the foregoing is the new Regulation No. 72 (11 NYCRR 174) promulgated by me on the 11th day of December, 1974.

BENJAMIN R. SCHENCK
Superintendent of Insurance

Dated: December 11, 1974

Date: Apr. 8, 1974
In reply to:
T:I:I:2:3

MR. MATTHEW J. ZINN
Steptoe and Johnson
1250 Connecticut Avenue, N.W.
  Suite 800
Washington, D. C. 20036

Dear Mr. Zinn:

This is in further reply to your ruling requests of December 18, 1972, and sub-sequent information submitted on May 16, 1973 and February 7, 1974. In our ruling of September 7, 1973, we addressed all of the ruling requests in your letter of December 18, 1972, relating to the Federal income tax consequences of various transactions in options purchased and sold through the Chicago Board Options Exchange, Inc. (the "CBOE") except those transactions involving "straddles" and those transactions designated as "closing transactions." This ruling addresses itself to the tax consequences of "closing transactions" which are described in this letter and which were your ruling requests designated B-4 and D-4. This ruling does not address itself to the tax consequences of "straddles" which ruling requests were contained in section E of your ruling request. We reserve the treatment of those pending submission of further information.

The issue herein resolved is as follows:

Does the writer of an option recognize ordinary income or loss, or capital gain or loss upon the payment of an amount equal to the market price of an equivalent option in exchange for the termination of the writer's obligation?

The CBOE is a Delaware nonstock corporation established to provide a national market in stock option contracts. The Chicago Board Options Exchange Clearing Corporation (OCC), a wholly owned subsidiary of CBOE, will serve as the clearing house for all CBOE transactions.

Option contracts, commonly known as "puts" and "calls," are agreements in which a writer offers to buy (in a "put") or sell (in a "call") specified amounts of named stock for a specified amount; the holder or purchaser of the offer, pays an amount (the "premium") in exchange for the writer's promise to hold the offer open for a specified period.

Before the CBOE was formed, all option contracts on stock were traded on the informal "over the counter" market. The terms of such options varied, and the writer of each option was contractually bound to the holder of that option.

In order to create an orderly market in options, the CBOE has standardized its option form, so that two options with the same expiration date and striking price are interchangeable. It has also severed the direct contractual tie between the writer and holder of the option, by having the option writers obligate themselves to the OCC, which in turn issues option contracts, on which it is obligated, to the holders, as the means of executing all sales made on the CBOE at the current market price. Thus, for each option contract sold, there will be a holder, upon whose election the OCC will be obligated to perform by completing the sale, and a writer, to whom the OCC in turn will look for performance if the holder so elects. No particular holder's option is identified with any particular writer however.

Because of the interchangeability of contracts of both writers and holders with the OCC, and the continuous market in such contracts, the OCC will allow either the writer or the holder of an option to terminate his contract, and thus fix his gain or loss. The holder of an OCC option who wishes to close out his position does so by selling his option contract through the OCC at the prevailing market price. As stated in holdings A-2 and C-2 of our September 7, 1973, ruling letter, gain or loss recognized by the holder in such a transaction is capital gain or loss, and is long term or short term depending on the period for which the option was held by the selling holder. Sections 1222 and 1234(a) of the Internal Revenue Code of 1954 (the "Code").

The writer of an option may also close out his position, by purchasing an OCC option of similar terms in a declared "closing transactions." However, when a writer enters into such a "closing transaction," he does not thereby become a holder of an option. He must designate his transaction *ab initio* as a "closing transaction" and thus acquires nothing more than he possessed as a writer before entering into the "closing transaction" other than the release from his obligation to perform if called upon to do so by the holder. If this is done, the OCC has agreed to substitute the obligation of the writer of the option purchased in place of that of the closing writer. Any difference between the amount received by the writer on the writing of the initial option ("premium") and the amount he must pay to purchase an equivalent option at the market price when he chooses to close out his position is gain or loss to the writer.

A determination of whether the writer of an option realizes capital gain or loss or ordinary income or loss in a "closing transaction" must rest on an analysis of what the writer is conveying.

An option is a contract under which the writer agrees to sell certain property, in this case corporate stock, usually for a designated price, to the holder, and to hold the offer open for a stated period. In exchange for this promise, the holder conveys some valuable consideration (the "premium"). When the requested consideration has been given, the option becomes a unilateral contract, having been fully performed by the holder. The remaining performance on the part of the writer consists of holding open the specified offer until the end of the period agreed upon, when the option lapses and the offer is withdrawn, or, if the holder accepts the offer, the offer and acceptance create a contract of sale to which the writer is bound.

181

The writer of an option has freedom in specifying the terms of his offer of purchase or sale, and the terms of his agreement to hold his offer open. However, once the requested consideration has been paid by a holder, the choice as to whether the purchase will be executed rests solely in the holder to become bound to the sale terms. Thus the only remaining interest of a writer of an unexercised option for which the holder has given consideration is an obligation to continue his offer under the terms specified.

When a CBOE option is sold under the facts described, the writer offers to buy or sell stock and to keep his offer open to the OCC for a specified period; the OCC in turn issues a similar offer to the holder. In exchange for the option, the holder pays the OCC a premium that the OCC in turn pays to the writer. Thus as to the holder, the OCC is the writer, and as to the writer, the OCC is the holder. In all other respects, however, the CBOE option is fundamentally identical to any other option contract.

If a writer purchases another writer's option having the same terms as his own, and signifies the purchase as a "closing transaction," the OCC will accept the other writer's obligation in place of that of the purchasing writer. The effect of this transaction is to eliminate the withdrawing writer's obligation to the OCC and to cause him to recognize gain or loss, depending on whether the premium he pays on the closing option purchase is more or less than the premium he received on the sale of his option.

Once the premium has been paid, an option contract becomes unilateral in that the holder has fully performed his part of the agreement. It must necessarily follow that the writer, as the other party to the contract, has no further right that might be enforced or protected under that agreement. Thus the writer has no capital asset to surrender in the "closing transaction." The writer does not exchange a right to sell the underlying stock to either the OCC or to the writer of the substituted option, because the withdrawing writer has no right under the contract to force the holder to buy or sell the underlying stock. The writer's only interest in the option contract is his obligation to keep the offer open. Such an obligation is not a capital asset. See *J. J. Shea,* 36 T.C. 577, 581 (1961), *aff'd* per curiam 327 F. 2d 1002 (5th Cir. 1964), holding that a guarantee of a corporation's debts is not a capital asset to the guarantor. Thus we do not believe that a closing transaction can be characterized as a sale or exchange of a capital asset.

In addition to the fact that the closing writer is transferring no "capital asset" within section 1221 of the Code, the closing transaction does not result in capital gain or loss because it does not involve a "sale or exchange." Even if the premium were to be paid at the end of the option period, the release of the right to receive it by the closing writer to the OCC would result in the extinguishment of that right. A release and extinguishment of a contract right is not a "sale or exchange" under section 1221 of the Code. See *Bingham v. Commissioner* 105 F. 2d 1971 (2d Cir. 1939); *Commissioner v. Starr Bros.* 204 F. 2d 673 (2d Cir. 1953); *General Artists Corp. v. Commissioner* 205 F. 2d 360 (2d Cir.) *cert. denied,* 346 U.S. 866 (1953); Rev. Rul. 56-531, 1956-2, C.B. 983; Rev. Rul. 58-394, 1958-2, C.B. 374.

Based on the above facts, representations, and the authorities and reasoning cited, we do not believe that the writer of an option has any contract right to the stock subject to the option, or to payment for such stock. Thus in a closing transaction, the writer could not convey a capital asset. We therefore conclude that the gain or loss recognized on such a transaction results in ordinary income or loss. More specifically we hold as follows:

1. If a writer of a call engages in a closing transaction by payment of an amount equivalent to the value of the call at the time of such payment, the difference between the amount so paid and the premium received by him is ordinary income or loss.

2. If the writer of a put engages in a closing transaction by payment of an amount equivalent to the value of the put at the time of such payment, the difference between the amount so paid and the premium received by him is ordinary income or loss.

Sincerely yours,
MILTON LICHTMAN
Acting Chief, Individual Income Tax Branch

Bibliography

AITCHISON, J. and J. A. C. BROWN: *The Lognormal Distribution* (London: Cambridge University Press, 1957).

ALVERSON, LYLE T.: *How to Write Puts and Calls* (Jericho, N. Y.: Exposition Press, 1968).

ANSBACHER, MAX G.: *The New Options Market* (New York: Walker & Co., 1975).

ARISTOTLE: *The Works of Aristotle. Vol. X, Politics.* J. A. Smith and W. D. Ross, ed. (London: Oxford University Press, 1921).

ARMSTRONG, T. H.: "Stock Purchase Warrants," *Analysts Journal,* May 1954, pp. 89-91.

ARROW, KENNETH: "The role of Securities in the Optimal Allocation of Risk-Bearing," *Review of Economic Studies,* April 1964, pp. 91-95.

ASEN, ROBERT and R. SCOTT ASEN: *How to Make Money Selling Stock Options* (West Nyack, N. Y.: Parker, 1970).

AYRES, HERBERT F.: "Risk Aversion in the Warrant Markets," *Industrial Management Review,* Fall 1963, pp. 45-53, reprinted in Paul H. Cootner, ed., *The Random Character of Stock Market Prices* (Cambridge, Mass.: M.I.T. Press, 1964), pp. 497-505.

BACHELIER, LOUIS: *Theory of Speculation* (translation of 1900 French edition), pp. 17-78 in Paul H. Cootner, ed. *The Random Character of Stock Market Prices* (Cambridge, Mass.: M.I.T. Press, 1964), pp. 17-68.

BAUMOL, WILLIAM J., BURTON G. MALKIEL, and RICHARD E. QUANDT: "An Organized Option Market and the Public Interest" in Vol. 2, Robert R. Nathan Associates, ed. *Public Policy Aspects of a Futures-Type Market in Options on Securities* (Chicago: Chicago Board of Trade, 1969).

BAUMOL, WILLIAM J., BURTON G. MALKIEL, and RICHARD E. QUANDT: "The Valuation of Convertible Securities," *Quarterly Journal of Economics,* Feb. 1966, pp. 48-59.

BERNOULLI, DANIEL: "Exposition of a New Theory on the Measurement of Risk," 1738 (translated from the Latin), in *Econometrica,* Jan. 1954, pp. 23-36.

Bible—Genesis 29, 30 and 41.

BIERMAN, HAROLD, JR.: *Financial Policy Decisions* (New York: Macmillan, 1970).

BIERMAN, HAROLD, JR.: "The Valuation of Stock Options," *Journal of Financial and Quantitative Analysis,* Sept. 1967, pp. 327-334.

BIRD, A. P.: "Evaluating Warrants," *The Investment Analyst,* Dec. 1971, pp. 17-32.

BLACK, FISCHER, MICHAEL C. JENSEN, and MYRON SCHOLES: "The Capital Asset Pricing Model: Some Empirical Tests," in Michael C. Jensen, ed. *Studies in the Theory of Capital Markets* (New York: Praeger, 1972).

BLACK, FISCHER and MYRON SCHOLES: "The Pricing of Options and Corporate Liabilities," *Journal of Political Economy,* May-June 1973, pp. 637-653.

BLACK, FISCHER and MYRON SCHOLES: "The Valuation of Option Contracts and a Test of Market Efficiency," *Journal of Finance,* May 1972, pp. 399-417.

BONESS, A. JAMES: "Elements of a Theory of Stock-Option Value," *Journal of Political Economy,* April 1964, pp. 163-175.

BONESS, A. JAMES: "Some Evidence on the Profitability of Trading in Put and Call Options," in Paul H. Cootner, ed. *The Random Character of Stock Market Prices* (Cambridge, Mass.: M.I.T. Press), 1964, pp. 475-496.

BOOKBINDER, ALBERT I. A.: "Appreciating Options," *Barron's,* June 15, 1964.

BOOKBINDER, ALBERT I. A.: *Investment Decision-Making* (Elmont, N. Y.: Programmed Press, 1968).

BRACKEN, JEROME: "Models for Call Option Decisions," *Financial Analysts Jour-*

187

nal, Sept. 1968, pp. 149-151.

BREALEY, RICHARD A.: *An Introduction to Risk and Return from Common Stocks* (Cambridge, Mass.: M.I.T. Press, 1969).

BREALEY, RICHARD A.: *Security Prices in a Competitive Market: More About Risk and Return from Common Stocks* (Cambridge, Mass.: M.I.T. Press, 1971).

BUSKIRK, RICHARD H. and BENJAMIN R. HOWE: *Preplanning a Profitable Call Writing Program* (Larchmont, N. Y.: Investors Intelligence, 1970).

CAMPANELLA, FRANK B.: *The Measurement of Portfolio Risk Exposure: Use of the Beta Coefficient* (Lexington, Mass.: D. C. Heath, 1972).

CASTELLI, CHARLES: *The Theory of Options in Stocks and Shares* (London: Mathieson, 1877).

CHEN, ANTHONY H. Y.: "A Model of Warrant Pricing in a Dynamic Market," *Journal of Finance*, December 1970, pp. 1041-1060.

CHENG, PAO L. and DONALD T. SAVAGE: "Short-Run Manipulative Aspects of Common Stock Warrants," *Quarterly Review of Economics and Business*, Summer 1963, pp. 102-107.

Chicago Board Options Exchange. *Option Writing Strategies* (Chicago: Chicago Board Options Exchange, 1975).

Chicago Board Options Exchange. *Options Trading on the Chicago Board Options Exchange* (Chicago: Chicago Board Options Exchange, 1973).

Chicago Board Options Exchange. *Understanding Options* (Chicago: Chicago Board Options Exchange, 1974).

CLASING, HENRY K., JR.: *Dow Jones-Irwin Guide to Put and Call Options* (Homewood, Ill.: Dow Jones-Irwin, 1975).

CLOONAN, JAMES B.: *Stock Options: The Application of Decision Theory to Basic and Advanced Strategies* (Chicago: Quantitative Decision Systems, 1973).

COOTNER, PAUL H. ed.: *The Random Character of Stock Market Prices* (Cambridge, Mass.: M.I.T. Press, 1964).

CPA Journal: "Tax Planning with CBOE Options," Aug. 1974, pp. 45-46.

CRESTOL, JACK, HERMAN M. SCHNEIDER and WARREN G. WINTRUB: *Investor's Tax Savings Guide* (Princeton, N. J.: Dow Jones Books, 1970).

CRESSON, GEORGE V.: "The Writing of Options," *Analysts Journal*, May 1959, pp. 43-46.

CUNNION, JOHN D.: *How to Get Maximum Leverage from Puts and Calls* (Larchmont, N. Y.: Business Reports, 1967).

DADEKIAN, ZAVEN A.: *The Strategy of Puts and Calls* (New York: Scribner's, 1968).

ELTON, E. J. and M. J. GRUBER: "The Economic Value of the Call Option," *Journal of Finance*, Sept. 1972, pp. 891-901.

FAMA, EUGENE F.: "The Behavior of Stock-Market Prices," *Journal of Business*, Jan. 1965, pp. 34-105.

FILER, HERBERT: "Investing in Options," *Analysts Journal*, Feb. 1955, pp. 77-78.

FILER, HERERT: *Understanding Put and Call Options* (New York: Crown Publishers, 1959).

Financial Research Center. *Research Memorandum No. 1* (Princeton, N. J.: Princeton University Press, 1968).

FISHER, LAWRENCE: "Outcomes for Random Investments in Common Stocks Listed on the New York Stock Exchange," *Journal of Business*, April 1965, pp. 149-161.

FISHER, LAWRENCE and JAMES H. LORIE: "Rates of Return on Investments in Common Stock," *Journal of Business*, Jan. 1964, pp. 1-17.

188

FISHER, LAWRENCE and JAMES H. LORIE: "Rates of Return on Investments in Common Stock. The Year by Year Record, 1926-65," *Journal of Business*, July 1968, pp. 291-316.

FISHER, LAWRENCE and JAMES H. LORIE: "Some Studies of Variability of Returns in Common Stocks," *Journal of Business*, April 1970, pp. 99-134.

FRANKLIN, C. B. and M. R. COLBERG: "Puts and Calls: A Factual Survey," *Journal of Finance*, March 1958, pp. 21-34.

FRANKLIN, C. B. and M. R. COLBERG: "Comment on Puts and Calls: A Factual Survey: Reply," *Journal of Finance*, March 1959, pp. 71-74.

FRIED, SIDNEY: *The Speculative Merits of Common Stock Warrants* (New York: RHM Associates, 1960).

GALLAGHER, THOMAS J., JR. and CLINTON M. TARKOE: "Taxing an Option on American Business: Puts, Calls and the IRC," *Taxes*, Aug. 1974, pp. 481-498.

GIGUERE, GUYNEMER: "Warrants—A Mathematical Method of Evaluation," *Analysts Journal*, Nov. 1958, pp. 17-25.

GROSS, LEROY: *The Stockbroker's Guide to Put and Call Option Strategies* (New York: New York Institute of Finance, 1974).

HALLINGBY, PAUL, JR.: "Speculative Opportunities in Stock Purchase Warrants," *Analysts Journal*, Vol. 3. No. 3, 1947, pp. 41-49.

HAUSMAN, W. H. and W. L. WHITE: "Theory of Option Strategy under Risk Aversion," *Journal of Financial and Quantitative Analysis*, September 1968, pp. 343-358.

HESSLEIN, MAX: *Puts and Calls* (New York: Put and Call Brokers and Dealers Association, 1934).

HESTER, DONALD and JAMES TOBIN ed.: *Risk Aversion and Portfolio Choice* (New York: Wiley, 1967).

HIGGINS, LEONARD R.: *The Put—and—Call* (London: Effingham Wilson, 1906).

HUBBARD, CHARLES L. and TERRY JOHNSON: "Profits from Writing Calls with Convertible Bonds," *Financial Analysts Journal*, Nov. 1969, pp. 78-79.

Investors' Chronicle, "All About Options," *Investors' Chronicle and Money Market Review*, Part 1: Sept. 1, 1961, pp. 757-758; Part 2: Sept. 8, 1961, pp. 838-839; and Part 3: Sept. 15, 1961, pp. 924-925.

JENSEN, MICHAEL C.: "Risk, the Pricing of Capital Assets, and the Evaluation of Investment Portfolios," *Journal of Business*, April 1969, pp. 167-247.

JENSEN, MICHAEL C. ed.: *Studies in the Theory of Capital Markets* (New York: Praeger, 1972).

KASSOUF, SHEEN T.: "An Econometric Model for Option Price," *Econometrica*, Oct. 1969, pp. 685-694.

KASSOUF, SHEEN T.: *Evaluation of Convertible Securities* (Brooklyn, N. Y.: Analytical Publishers, 1969).

KASSOUF, SHEEN T.: *A Theory and an Econometric Model for Common Stock Purchase Warrants*. Ph.D. Dissertation, Columbia University (Brooklyn, N. Y.: Analytical Publishers, 1965).

KASSOUF, SHEEN T.: "Warrant Price Behavior—1945 to 1964," *Financial Analysts Journal*, Jan.-Feb. 1968, pp. 123-126.

KATZ, RICHARD: "The Profitability of Put and Call Option Writing," *Industrial Management Review*, Fall 1963, pp. 55-69.

KRUIZENGA, RICHARD J.: "Comment on Puts and Calls: A Factual Survey," *Journal of Finance*, March 1950, pp. 67-70.

KRUIZENGA, RICHARD J.: "Introduction to the Option Contract," in Paul H. Cootner, ed. *The Random Character of Stock Market Prices* (Cambridge, Mass.: M.I.T. Press, 1964), pp. 377-391.

189

KRUIZENGA, RICHARD J.: "Profit Returns from Purchasing Puts and Calls," in Paul H. Cootner, ed. *The Random Character of Stock Market Prices* (Cambridge, Mass.: M.I.T. Press, 1964), pp. 392-411.

KRUIZENGA, RICHARD J.: *Put and Call Options: A Theoretical and Market Analysis* (unpublished doctoral dissertation), Massachusetts Institute of Technology, 1956.

KUHN, C. RICHARD: "Using Call Options to Improve Trust Investment Performance, Trusts & Estates," April 1973.

LAERTIUS, DIOGENES: *Lives of Eminent Philosophers* (translation) (Cambridge, Mass.: Harvard University Press, 1959), Thales, pp. 22-45.

LAYNE, ABNER A: "Want to Stretch Stock Profits? Try Writing Options," *Medical Economics*, Oct. 25, 1971.

LORIE, JAMES H. and MARY T. HAMILTON: *The Stock Market: Theories and Evidence* (Homewood, Ill.: Richard D. Irwin, 1973).

MALKIEL, BURTON G.: "Put and Call Options," *Wall Street Transcript*, Oct. 26, 1972, pp. 30,810-30,812.

MALKIEL, BURTON G.: *A Random Walk Down Wall Street* (New York: W. W. Norton, 1973).

MALKIEL, BURTON G.: "Trading in Options: What Are the Best Strategies?" *Commercial and Financial Chronicle*, Dec. 14, 1972, pp. 1 and 12.

MALKIEL, BURTON G. and RICHARD E. QUANDT: "Can Options Improve an Institution's Performance?" *Institutional Investor*, Nov. 1968, pp. 55-57, 101-103.

MALKIEL, BURTON G. and RICHARD E. QUANDT: *Strategies and Rational Decisions in the Securities Options Market* (Cambridge, Mass.: M.I.T. Press, 1969).

MARKOWITZ, HARRY: "Portfolio Selection," *Journal of Finance*, March 1952, pp. 77-91.

MARKOWITZ, HARRY M.: *Portfolio Selection: Efficient Diversification of Investments* (New Haven, Conn.: Yale University Press, 1959).

McGUIGAN, J. R. and W. R. KING: "Security Option Strategy under Risk Aversion," *Journal of Financial and Quantitative Analysis*, Jan. 1973, pp. 1-15.

MERTON, ROBERT C.: "Theory of Rational Option Pricing," *Bell Journal of Economics and Management Science*, Spring 1973, pp. 141-183.

MILLER, JARROTT T.: *Options Trading* (Chicago: Henry Regnery Co., 1975).

MILLER, JERRY D.: "Effects of Longevity on Values of Stock Purchase Warrants," *Financial Analyst Journal*, Nov.-Dec. 1971, pp. 78-85.

MILLER, MERTON H.: "The Effects of an Improved Option Market on the Costs of Debt and of Equity Capital," in Vol. 2, Robert R. Nathan Associates, ed. *Public Policy Aspects of a Futures-Type Market in Options on Securities* (Chicago: Chicago Board of Trade, 1969).

MORRISON, R. J.: "The Warrants or the Stock?" *Analysts Journal*, November 1957, pp. 51-52.

NATHAN, ROBERT R. ed.: *Public Policy Aspects of a Futures-Type Market in Options on Securities* (Chicago: Chicago Board of Trade, 1969).

NATHAN, ROBERT R. ed.: *Review of Initial Trading Experience at the Chicago Board Options Exchange* (Chicago: Chicago Board Options Exchange, Dec. 1974).

NODDINGS, THOMAS C.: *The Dow Jones-Irwin Guide to Convertible Securities* (Homewood, Ill.: Dow-Jones-Irwin, 1973).

NODDINGS, THOMAS C. and EARL ZAZOVE: *Listed Call Options: Your Daily Guide to Portfolio Strategy* (Homewood, Ill.: Dow Jones-Irwin, 1975).

OPPENHEIM, APPEL, DIXON & Co.: *Tax Considerations in Using CBOE Options* (Chicago: Chicago Board Options Exchange, 1975).

PACEY, MARGARET D.: "Option Pick-Up," *Barron's*, September 22, 1969.

PARKINSON, MICHAEL: "Empirical Warrant-Stock Relationships," *Journal of Business*, Oct. 1972, pp. 563-569.

PEASE, F.: "The Warrant—Its Power and Its Hazards," *Financial Analysts Journal*, Jan.-Feb. 1963, pp. 25-32.

PLATT, S. D. and D. A. ROSEN: "Put and Call Options under Section 16 of the Securities Exchange Act," *Yale Law Journal*, Apr. 1960, pp. 868-894.

PLUM, V. L. and T. J. MARTIN: "The Significance of Conversion Parity in Valuing Common Stock Warrants," *The Financial Review*, February 1966.

PRATT, JOHN W.: "Risk Aversion in the Small and in the Large," *Econometrica*, Jan.-April 1964, pp. 122-136.

PRATT SHANNON: "Relationships Between Risk and Rate of Return for Common Stock" (Indiana University dissertation, 1966), in James H. Lorie and Mary T. Hamilton, *The Stock Market: Theories and Evidence* (Homewood, Ill.: Richard D. Irwin, 1973), pp. 215-226.

PRENDERGAST, S. LAWRENCE: *Uncommon Profits through Stock Purchase Warrants* (Homewood, Ill.: Dow Jones-Irwin, 1973).

PUGLISI, DONALD J.: "A Rationale for Option Buyer Behavior: Theory and Evidence," *Quarterly Review of Economics and Business*, Spring 1974, pp. 55-65.

REINACH, ANTHONY M.: *The Nature of Puts and Calls* (New York: Bookmailer, 1961).

ROSEN, LAWRENCE R.: *How to Trade Put and Call Options* (Homewood, Ill.: Dow Jones-Irwin, 1974).

ROSETT, RICHARD N.: "Estimating the Utility of Wealth from Call Options Data," in Donald D. Hester and James Tobin, ed. *Risk Aversion and Portfolio Choice* (New York: Wiley, 1967).

SAMUELSON, PAUL A.: "Rational Theory of Warrant Pricing," *Industrial Management Review*, Spring 1965, pp. 13-32.

SAMUELSON, PAUL A. and ROBERT C. MERTON: "A Complete Model of Warrant Pricing that Maximizes Utility," *Industrial Management Review*, Winter 1969, pp. 17-46.

SARNOFF, PAUL: *Puts and Calls: The Complete Guide* (New York: Hawthorne, 1968).

SCHOLES, MYRON: "Rational Option Pricing and Price Movements on the CBOE," in *Review of Initial Option Trading Experience at the Chicago Board Options Exchange*, Robert R. Nathan, ed. (Chicago: Chicago Board Options Exchange, Dec. 1974), Appendix B.

SHARPE, WILLIAM F.: *Portfolio Theory and Capital Markets* (New York: McGraw-Hill, 1970).

SHELTON, JAMES P.: "The Relation of the Pricing of a Warrant to the Price of Its Associated Stock," *Financial Analysts Journal*, May-June 1967 and July-August 1967.

SMITH, KEITH V.: "Option Writing and Portfolio Management," *Financial Analysts Journal*, May-June 1968, pp. 135-138.

SNYDER, GERARD L.: "Alternative Forms of Options," *Financial Analysts Journal*, Sept.-Oct. 1969, pp. 93-100.

SNYDER, GERARD: "A Look at Options," *Financial Analysts Journal*, Jan. 1967, pp. 100-103.

SPRENKLE, CASE M.: "Warrant Prices as Indicators of Expectations and Preferences," *Yale Economic Essays*, 1961, pp. 179-231, reprinted in Paul H. Cootner, ed., *The Random Character of Stock Market Prices* (Cambridge, Mass.: M.I.T. Press, 1964), pp. 412-474.

STOLL, HANS REINER: "The Relationship Between Put and Call Option Prices," *Journal of Finance*, December 1969, pp. 801-824.

SULLIVAN, JOSEPH W. and BURTON G. MALKIEL: "Options Seminar" at the New York Society of Security Analysts (Chicago, Ill.: Chicago Board Options Exchange, Oct. 26, 1972).

SULLIVAN, JOSEPH W.: "Put and Call Options" (speech before the New York Society of Security Analysts), *Wall Street Transcript*, Nov. 20, 1972, p. 30, 810.

TAYLOR, HOWARD M.: "Evaluating a Call Option and Optimal Timing Strategy in the Stock Market," *Management Science*, Sept. 1967, pp. 111-120.

THORP, EDWARD O. and SHEEN T. KASSOUF: *Beat the Market* (New York: Random House, 1967).

TUROV, DANIEL: "Dividend Paying Stocks and Their Warrants," *Financial Analysts Journal*, March-April 1963.

TUROV, DANIELS "New Look in Calls: Chicago Options Exchange Is Really Dealing in Warrants," *Barron's*, Aug. 6, 1973.

Twentieth Century Fund: *The Security Markets* (New York: Twentieth Century Fund, 1935).

U.S. Securities and Exchange Commission: *Report on Put and Call Options* (Washington: U.S. Government Printing Office, August 1961).

U.S. Internal Revenue Service: *Internal Revenue Code*, 1954.

U.S. Senate, Stock Exchange Practices, Hearings Before the Committee on Banking and Currency, 73rd Congress, 1st & 2nd sessions, 1933.

U.S. Senate, Stock Exchange Practices, Senate Report 1455, 1934.

VAN HORNE, JAMES C.: "Warrant Valuation in Relation to Volatility and Opportunity Costs," *Industrial Management Review*, Spring 1969, pp. 19-32.

VON NEUMANN, JOHN and OSKAR MORGENSTERN: *Theory of Games* (New York: Wiley, 1964).

WHITING, RICHARD: *Profitable Trading with Puts and Calls* (New York: RHM Associates, 1960).

WHITTAKER, JOHN: "The Evaluation of Warrants," *Investment Analyst*, Oct. 1967, pp. 39-47.

WILLIAMS, JOHN BURR: *The Theory of Investment Value* (Cambridge, Mass.: Harvard University Press, 1938).

WOLLIN, GARY A.: "Call Options Revisited—the CBOE—Its Effect on Rate of Return," *Trusts and Estates*, Jan. 1974, pp. 26-29, 58.

ZIEG, KERMIT C.: *The Profitability of Stock Options* (Larchmont, N. Y.: Investors Intelligence, 1970).

Index

Index

INDEX

197

198

THE AUTHOR

Albert I. A. Bookbinder received his Master of Arts degree from Columbia University and also did graduate work at the University of Pennsylvania. He was awarded the Doctor of Philosophy degree by Fordham University.

Dr. Bookbinder was Financial Statistician of the Securities and Exchange Commission, Research Director of New York Stock Exchange member firms and Investment Manager of a group of foundations.

The author's numerous publications have appeared in such leading periodicals as *Barron's, The Financial Analysts Journal, The Commercial and Financial Chronicle* and the *Journal of Finance*. His books include INVESTMENT DECISION-MAKING as well as SECURITY OPTIONS STRATEGY.

Dr. Bookbinder has been Adjunct Professor of the Graduate School of Business at Fordham University and is Professor of Economics at the City University of New York. He acts as investment counselor for selected clients.